T0169125

SHAMAN PATHWAYS

Following the Deer Trods

A practical guide to working
with Elen of the Ways

SHAMAN PATHWAYS

Following the Deer Trods

A practical guide to working
with Elen of the Ways

Elen Sentier

Winchester, UK
Washington, USA

First published by Moon Books, 2014
Moon Books is an imprint of John Hunt Publishing Ltd., Laurel House, Station Approach,
Alresford, Hants, SO24 9JH, UK
office1@jhpbooks.net
www.johnhuntpublishing.com
www.moon-books.net

For distributor details and how to order please visit the 'Ordering' section on our website.

Text copyright: Elen Sentier 2014

ISBN: 978 1 78279 826 2
Library of Congress Control Number: 2014948061

All rights reserved. Except for brief quotations in critical articles or reviews, no part of this
book may be reproduced in any manner without prior written permission from the publishers.

The rights of Elen Sentier as author have been asserted in accordance with the Copyright,
Designs and Patents Act 1988.

A CIP catalogue record for this book is available from the British Library.

Design: Stuart Davies
www.stuartdaviesart.com

Printed and bound by CPI Group (UK) Ltd, Croydon, CR0 4YY

We operate a distinctive and ethical publishing philosophy in all
areas of our business, from our global network of authors to
production and worldwide distribution.

CONTENTS

Dedication

Go into this journey full of expectancy but with no expectations ...

1

Deer Trods

Following the deer trods is to walk the path of the awenydd in Britain.

Deer trods are the footprints of deer, the cloven-hoof prints you sometimes see when out walking in wild places. They are one of the tracker's signs that deer are in the neighbourhood; they can also tell how long ago the deer were there, the size of the animals, perhaps something about their gender and species, which way they were going, whether they were running or walking or jumping. They are full of information if we can only read it. In this book they refer specifically to the footprints of Elen of the Ways, the deer goddess. Working with them we can learn about life, the universe and everything.

Elen is known to have been part of our lives here in Britain for more than 14,000 years. A reindeer engraved on the wall of a cave in South Wales was found to date from at least 14,505 years ago. This makes this reindeer the oldest rock art in the British Isles, if not North-West Europe.

In September 2010 Dr George Nash from the University of Bristol Department of Archaeology and Anthropology discovered the carving at the rear of the Cathole Cave in South Wales on a small vertical limestone niche. It is a stylised reindeer, drawn side-on and carved with a sharp-pointed tool, probably made of flint, by an artist using his or her right hand. The reindeer's elongated torso has been cross-hatched with vertical and diagonal lines, while the legs and stylised antlers comprise simple lines. Such technique argues serious artistic ability.

So our British ancestors, of more than 14,500 years ago, were skilled artists ... with all that implies.

So far this is the earliest rendition we have discovered, but that doesn't mean it *is* the earliest, it's quite possible archaeologists will discover even older mentions of the reindeer. Elen has probably been part of our lives from the dawn of human times, since we first followed the reindeer, although there is no archaeology as yet discovered to "prove" it.

Elen is an antlered goddess. The only female deer who carry antlers are the reindeer. They are ancient and once, more than 8,000 years ago, ran all over Britain. In those days we were still a forested country and actively part of the Boreal Forest, the great forest that stretches all around the northern hemisphere from the tundra down to the latitude of Land's End in Cornwall. Since agriculture got going here in Britain some 6,000 years ago the forests have been cut down, the habitat changed and the reindeer gone, although a herd have been reintroduced in the Cairngorms.

The absence of forests and wild reindeer does not mean that Elen has left us too, she certainly has not! She is still here throughout the land, you find her name in springs, wells, place-names all over the country. They may turn up as Helen instead of Elen, the Christians took her over and changed her name, calling her St Helen, and messing and mulching with her stories, but she's still there. She's waiting for us to notice her again and ask to work with her.

This book guides you into the beginning of following in her footprints for yourself.

Old Custom ...

I was born on Dartmoor and grew up on Exmoor, my family followed the deer trods for generations. It was *custom* back then in the 1950s and was carried on quietly in many country places and some towns too all through Britain. Nobody talked about it much, it was just what you did. Not everyone followed the old ways then any more than they do now although there is a growing interest nowadays. People want to find the traditions of our own lands rather than always borrowing someone else's because it's better known and has been written about far more.

We're a funny old lot in this country, we riddle quite as well as Zen teachings and most of our lore – we call it grammarye – is hidden in stories and songs that require some work on the part of the reader/listener to discern what is really being said. My husband is a musician and much attracted to Mozart. He says of Mozart's music that it comes in layers; at the top is the pretty, catchy tune that you can hum along with; then there's the beauty of the way the whole thing is put together, the intricacy and the intimacy; then there's the deep stuff that Mozart put there, which calls the spirit *if you allow it to.*

The same goes for our grammarye. You can read the romanticised Victorian Mabinogion stories; you can attempt the academic descriptions and deciphering of them; or you can work with them yourself, perhaps with the help of someone who has gone there before and whom you trust, and see what the stories themselves have to gift you.

As I grew up my family and the elders of the village led some of us children through the ways of working with the old ways, and through the stories, with lots of experiential work that enabled us – if we wanted to – to go deeper and deeper in following the deer trods.

If you like to follow me through these pages we'll have a nice bimble through the world, inside, outside and all around the edges, getting to know everything as well as we can. It's possible to become very intimate with the ways; you come to know in your bones that you are never, ever alone. Always, when following the deer trods, you are surrounded by friends … if you will only look to notice them. And that's what learning to follow the deer trods is about, noticing, asking and listening … as you'll likely have already guessed if you've read some of my other books.

So here we go …

2

What is Following the Deer Trods?

Those of us who follow the deer trods in Britain are called *awenydd* in the old British language, Brythonic. Brython is the word from which our name, Britain, stems. Awenydd means spirit-keeper and comes from the word *awen*, which means spirit.

Awenyddion (the plural of awenydd) have served the British tribes for hundreds of thousands of years, as long as there have been humans living in our land. We call this path walking the deer trods ... following the ancient ways of the deer goddess as our ancestors did from Palaeolithic times. We still do the work now, in the 21st century, for everything that lives on the Earth and the Earth herself, the seen and unseen, the human and not-human. We journey to bring wisdom and enable healing for creatures, people, plants and the land herself.

In other traditions, and fairly generally around the world for the past 50-odd years, those who do this work have been known as shamans. The word *shaman* comes from the language of the Tunguska people who live in a region of Eastern Siberia. Their word shaman, which we now use to cover a multitude of peoples, means *one who knows*. In the British tongue we call this knowing *kenning* – think of the words of the folksong "D'ye ken John Peel?" – it means knowing and gives us another name for the people of the old ways, the cunning folk. The awenydd, the cunning one, the wise one, is someone who works in the ecstasy, who has fire in the head, someone who stimulates, animates, motivates and electrifies others. They journey out for their people and return bringing the wisdom.

We awenyddion honour the spirit of the Earth and work with the spirit of the land. For me, this involves all sorts of things from growing my own veg to politics as well as spirit walking, journeying and healing. For each awenydd the form of the path is different, but the purpose is always the same … working for Mother Earth and all the life that lives and breathes and has its movement therein. This is so whatever its species and includes rocks and soil and what many folk call inanimate life, even one's fridge or car. Everything on Earth, every atom and molecule, and the Earth herself is animate … everything has spirit.

Keeping Spirit

So what does it mean to keep spirit?

It's worth playing with the thesaurus to expand our minds from the small interpretations we're likely to have of words. What does the word *keep* mean, what do we do when we keep spirit? I find the most appropriate ideas are *honour, fulfil, observe* and *respect*; and to *be*. The awenydd *is* spirit as well as a human being incarnate on Earth. The *and/and* principle is fundamental for following the deer trods; things are not *either/or*, they are inclusive rather than exclusive.

Other words the thesaurus gives for the word "keep" are *preserve, retain, maintain, sustain* and *conserve*, all of which give very good ideas about the jobs the awenydd does.

In order to do this over the past couple of thousand years we awenyddion have also had to *hide, conceal* and *guard* the old ways. The old ways, the cunning ways, the wild magic has been regarded as bad and subversive by many of the peoples who've come to this land as conquerors; the Romans, Christians and Normans especially come to mind. Indeed, the old ways don't lend themselves readily to conformist forms of government or institutions as commended by those peoples.

We are pagans. The word pagan comes from the Latin *paganus* and means "of the land". We are indeed of the land. It is well and rightly said that to get a group of pagans to agree about anything is worse than attempting to herd cats! And so it should be.

The Romans were not all bad, but not all good either, they

sometimes took on our goddess and her guardian god under names they used at home; see the lord and lady who guard the springs at Bath for a good example of this.

Sul (Sulis, Sulei, Sulla) is a Brythonic, Gaulish and Galician goddess. Her name suggests various Indo-European words for "Sun". She is a healing goddess, associated with hot springs and sometimes known as the Bright One. Bath was called Aquae Sulis, meaning the waters of Sulis, by the Romans. They associated her with the goddess they called Minerva and thought of her as a solar deity. Sulis Minerva is one of the few attested pairings of a Celtic goddess with her Roman counterpart.

Figure 1: Green Man Sul

This carving was on the front of the temple at Bath. You can see wings and snakes around the head, it looks like the Greek Medusa, whose head was worn on Minerva's breastplate after she was killed by Perseus, so likely this is what the Romans thought it was. But the gorgon has a flowing moustache and hair sticking up in bunches, which is the style of a Celtic man. Warriors would smear lime in their hair to make it stand up.

It's far more likely that this is a representation of Beli, Belenus. Belenus is a Sun god from our Celtic mythos and called the "Fair Shining One". This aligns well with Sul who is also called the Bright One and whose name may derive from words for the Sun. The Romans associated him with Apollo.

The Romans did do their worst to upend our knowing though, by making the god superior to the goddess, a beginning of patriarchy. The old ways always have the goddess holding and granting sovereignty, not the god.

After the Romans, the Vikings and Anglo Saxons were not particularly religious bigots and often still seemed to have a foot in both camps. In those times too women held land, were judges, led and organised battles and were not chattels; and we still elected our kings. The old ways still had something of a place alongside the "new religion", Christianity.

The Christians, however, were absolute religious bigots and very cruel with it, many still are. Cruelty seems to be an integral part of all three of the Religions of the Book (the Bible) – Christianity, Judaism and Muslimism. With the advent of the Normans in 1066 they came into their full power and did their best to crush us.

The Normans were frightful and their legacy still exists today in our governmental structure, hierarchy, the concepts of landed gentry and birthright, primogeniture or the right, by law or custom, of the firstborn male child to inherit the family estate. Before the Normans we elected our rulers! The Normans also put the kybosh on women's rights; women became chattels, property to be bought and sold, a form of slavery. My great aunt, Ursula Mellor Bright, was a political activist in the women's suffrage campaign and her efforts were fundamental in bringing in the 1882 Married Women's Property Act; this is what really got the women's rights movement back on the road after the best part of a thousand years. Needless to say it runs in the blood!

So, for the past couple of thousand years, and especially the past thousand, we of the old ways have had to hide and pretend we don't exist in order to survive. Did you know the witchcraft act was only repealed in 1951? There is still quite a strong aversion to anything except "established religions" nowadays. The other Religions of the Book, i.e. Judaism and Muslimism, are now part of the group of established and acceptable faiths, along with Hinduism, although they may still get glances askance from many people. Anything pagan is definitely something to be wary of for most.

So being awenydd involves having the ability to *hide, conceal* and *guard* spirit as necessary.

What about *mind, sit-with* and *watch*? These are very much part of following the deer trods and something you'll learn as you walk through this book.

To *mind* something is to give it your attention, to notice it, observe it and recognise it. It's also about learning it, being aware of it, understanding it, making its acquaintance and coming to know it in your bones. Becoming acquainted with spirit and becoming friends with it is vital for the work.

To *sit with* something is part of it too. Sitting with is one of the first things you learn. Sitting with the spirit of something, and the actual physical thing as well when possible, and allowing it to show you things, tell you about itself, is another fundamental part of following the deer trods. It's a big listening skill that involves learning to sit and listen without interrupting or asking questions all the time and certainly not translating what you hear into what you think it means!

Watching is another vital skill. It too involves observing without translation, just seeing what is actually there without interpreting. You cannot learn if you have a head full of preconceptions.

Like shamans all around the world, we who follow the deer trods work from the kenning, which we hone with the techniques above. This knowing works within *the mind's eye*, and is about discovering things for yourself, internalising what you come to know, making things your own rather than quoting the book-learned opinions of other people.

As I said, the Tungus word *shaman* means *one who knows*. This knowing is difficult to describe, but I'll try with this story...

If I throw a bucket of water over you then you know you are wet. You don't need to read a book on it, go on a weekend course, get a degree ... you know, intrinsically, that you are wet. You're probably quite cross with me too! But you are certainly immersed in the whole experience of wetness and you know, without doubt, what it's like!

That's what I'm talking about; that absolute certainty that cannot be argued out of you by any intellectual means. This is *kenning*, and the ability to do it is called *nous* (pronounced nowse). The wisdom to know when it's appropriate to do something is called *gumption*; gumption is about knowing *when* and *how* to act, and *when* to leave well alone! It's strongly related to *common sense* which, unfortunately, is no longer at all common! None of these have much to do with the intellect, but absolutely masses to do with instinct and intuition, and that thing called *body-knowing*, which is another fundamental tool for following the deer trods.

Making Mistakes Successfully

The person who never made a mistake never made anything ... my dad said this to me when I was a wee kiddy and I've never forgotten it. It is just so useful and helpful to know that you may actually screw up, get things wrong, and be able to get over it without the whole universe collapsing on top of you.

Since I grew up Britain has very much bought into the American blame-culture; if something happens then it must be someone's fault and you should sue that person, blame them, incarcerate them ... there are no such things as accidents any more. Way back in the 1950s even dad said the world was getting to be run by that famous firm of solicitors ... Sooe, Gabbitt &

Runne. I think he had a point! Blame and guilt, along with not accepting that shit happens, certainly isn't useful for following the deer trods; making mistakes successfully is.

Getting into this blame-culture means you cannot make any mistakes and so you cannot learn from them. Think about that ... what do you remember best? When you got something right or when you got something wrong? When you get something wrong, and you are honest and open enough with yourself to accept it, you understand ...

- The thing you did wrong.
- The reasons why you got it wrong.
- The consequences of getting it wrong.
- How to get it right again, if possible.
- When it's so broke you must just leave it alone.

All of these things are invaluable in your everyday life and in your work with spirit.

Following the deer trods means you no longer have to work in a set of boxes ... one for work, one for being a mum or dad, one for the neighbours, one for weekends, one for doing spirit-stuff. The deer trods show you how everything is both spirit *and* matter at the same time, and that includes you. Making mistakes opens up boxes and doors that you likely never even thought of, that enable you to work in whole new ways.

Keep that always in mind. When you make a mistake, you remember. When everything goes along swimmingly you're not really concentrating, you don't focus, so you don't really learn. Making mistakes successfully offers the opportunity of learning from them.

So how do you make a mistake successfully?

- Be honest, admit it.
- Ask for help.

- Apologise to all those hurt by your mistake.
- Listen, watch and learn from those who help you.
- Don't sulk!
- Don't be ashamed and therefore afraid to admit it.
- Never, ever, ever, make nasty comments to or about anyone else who makes a mistake and admits it!

All along the path, whatever your level of experience, you *will* make mistakes, get things wrong; I still do after 65+ years. That's good ... while you're making mistakes and admitting them you will always be learning.

Otherworld beings know mistakes will happen, they just want us to learn from them. They will show you how to ...

- Learn from them.
- Say sorry.
- Pick up the pieces (or not!).
- Most of all, to ask your familiars and teachers how to deal with whatever happened in the most appropriate way for all concerned.

The first thing is to learn not to be afraid to admit that you've made the mistake. Otherworld does *not* expect perfection so don't even try to be perfect. Otherworld *will* help you out of the holes you find yourself in when you've realised that you're in a hole and have stopped digging! Learning not to dig yourself ever deeper into the hole is vital.

Then you need to learn when and how to clean up after the mistake. Otherworld will help you learn that too. The best way to begin is to say, "*Sorry! I screwed up!*" This shows Otherworld that you've got enough *nous* to know when you've screwed up and the *gumption*, the common sense, to admit it. The next thing to say is, "*What do I do about it?*"

Then you have to listen ...

3

Ways to Work with the Deer Trods

Before I go any further I'm going to give you two exercises that underpin all the work in this book and refer to everything I've said so far. They really do work and are very simple. If you begin to get them into your autopilot right now, you'll find them invaluable in every part of your life.

Sit-With Technique

This is a **listening skill**, you learn to listen with an open mind, not jumping to conclusions or making assumptions. You also learn to listen to things other than words.

Listening to Otherworld can be difficult at first.

Most people, when they listen to someone, are trying to "understand" and "make sense" of what they hear. This usually means fitting what they hear into some pre-learned box, turning what the person said into what they think the person means and it's almost certainly going to be wrong! This is manipulation ... of the person and their words ... to make you feel more comfortable with what you're hearing. It makes what you hear seem familiar, you feel you already know it so you are not frightened by "the unknown". So many of us are taught to fear what we don't know, as well as things that are different from ourselves and our expectations. These exercises will help you learn to just listen without having to manipulate what you hear to fit in with what you already know.

Practise the following ... you'll need a clock and a pen!

1. Take a word, any noun will do, and write it down on a clean sheet of paper.
2. Sit quiet with your word, *give it your full attention*, as if it

was your best beloved – for so it is.

3.   Give yourself *no more than* 10 minutes.

- Jot down *images, words and/or phrases* that come into your mind. These will be from the word itself, *if* you are giving it your full attention.
- Do *not* try to understand or make sense, just listen, see pictures, feel ...
- No "stream of consciousness" stuff either, just brief, succinct pictures and words/phrases.
- You may only get one or two images/words/phrases, that's fine. It's entirely unnecessary to write *War and Peace* for the word!

4.   **Stop** at 10 minutes, or before if you feel the off-switch go – get used to knowing when your own personal *on/off-switch* happens. Do *not* extend the time. Work in *quanta*, i.e. tiny packages rather than great big lumps.

5.   Have a cup of tea, do something else, something completely different, put the whole thing out of your conscious mind.

- This is very important! *Do not* worry at it like a terrier with a bone. To do this will clog up your unconscious, which is your microcosm of Lowerworld. When you clog up your own unconscious you also clog up a bit of the Universal Unconscious – because your little bit is a part of the greater one. What you do *here* affects *there*. The Universal Unconscious does *not* appreciate being clogged up!

When you've finished your tea, go back and *look at* (don't read! just look) your piece of paper and the images, words and phrases that came to you. *Absorb* them. Again, don't try to make sense, allow *digestion* and *incubation* to take place. Every now and then over the next few days go and look at the paper again, stir the pot so to speak. It will continue to boil and bubble in your cauldron and new drops of inspiration will leap out at you every now and again, probably when you least expect it.

You use this technique *all the time* in following the deer trods.

Earth/Sun Exercise

This exercise underpins all the work. If you make doing it a daily habit it will help you *know* the backbone of the web, the World Tree, through your own body, know it in your bones.

It's *very* grounding; it will anchor you to the Earth and – at the same time – enable you to reach out across the solar system to the Sun whose light and warmth enables life on Earth.

Try to do this exercise every day when you get up. You can also do it when you go to sleep at night, it will help your dreaming and recall. Practise doing it sitting or lying down as well as standing.

Read the script through several time so you get to know it and know what you're going to do. Do the exercise standing up; it helps you to feel it through your body.

- Stand relaxed, weight evenly on both feet.
- Make sure your back is *comfortably* straight, neither rigid nor in spasm. Forearms, wrists, hands, all relaxed. Neck and head comfortable, with a slight forward tilt to allow the energy to pass *down and up* your spine easily. You need to anchor to the Earth before you reach out into the solar system.
- Now … focus on your breathing, just allow the breath to flow in and out without any changes. This quiets you, takes you out of your head-space.
- When you feel quiet … imagine the heart of the Earth beneath you, the heart of the Sun above you and your own heart at the centre.

- See a thread of energy go *down* out of your heart centre, down the spine, down through the ground, down to the central fire at the *heart of the Earth*.
- See the thread of energy penetrate this fire at the *heart of the Earth* and be lit by a spark there.
- Now … see that spark, from the heart of the Earth, travel back *up* your thread, through the Earth, through the ground, up the spine and out through the top of your head.
- See the thread and the spark from the heart of the Earth travelling *up* through space, until they reach the heart of the Sun. See them enter the Sun and the Earth-spark be met by a spark from the heart of the Sun.
- See Earth-fire and Sun-fire meet and greet each other, see them join together.
- Now … Earth-fire leads Sun-fire back *down* your thread, across space, through your crown, down the spine and down to the heart of the Earth.
- Sun-fire grows brighter.
- Now … Sun-fire turns, leads Earth-fire back *up* through your spine, through your crown, across space and into the heart of the Sun.
- Earth-fire grows brighter.
- Now … Earth-fire turns, leads Sun-fire back *down* across space, through your crown, through your spine, and into the heart of the Earth.
- They dance, up and down, down and up. Each grows brighter with every passage.
- Spend time watching the conjoined sparks do this journey between the heart of the Earth and the heart of the Sun.
- Now … this time … as they arrive again in the Sun, see the pulsing movement gently slow and stop as the Earth-spark and Sun-spark kiss and part company again.
- The Sun-spark retires back into the heart of the Sun and

the Earth-spark flows back down your thread, down the spine, through you and into the heart of the Earth where it gently leaves go of your thread and retires into the smouldering fire of Earth.

- Now … gently withdraw your thread from the heart of the Sun. See, feel, the thread roll back down into your crown, down your spine, to curl into your heart.
- Now … gently withdraw your thread from the heart of the Earth. See, feel, the thread roll back up into your body, up your spine, to curl into your heart.
- Feel yourself disengage from Otherworld, back in your everyday-self.
- Feel the ground beneath you, reach down and touch it, rub your hands on it. Rub your knees, your feet, then rub your hands together. Rub your body, arms, legs, neck, and head. Roll your head on your neck. Yawn. Breathe deeply in, then blow the breath out hard, do this again … and again. Roll your tongue around your mouth, lick your lips. Open your eyes, roll your eyes around and focus on something near, then something further off. Roll your shoulders. Stretch your arms. Arch your back then bend forward. Finally slide onto the ground and lie in the foetal position for a few minutes, reconnecting with the Earth.
- Know yourself to be here … and know where here is!

Now you've done the exercise go eat, drink and give yourself some treats. Then, when you feel ready, make drawings and notes, look back over the exercise.

These simple-seeming exercises are the skeleton and structure on which all the work of following the deer trods is built. I was lucky and learned them practically from the cradle so they are well in my bones. That doesn't matter though, everyone can learn them and everyone benefits from them. You can use them in all sorts of situations ... and remember, all of life is *both* spirit and matter; the two are intertwined and two sides of one coin.

Foot Dowsing

Deer trods are footprints. There are stories around the world of people whose footprints, when they walk, have energy. One of the most famous is the story of Wenceslas who we sing about as a Christmas carol ...

Mark my footsteps, my good page
Tread thou in them boldly
Thou shalt find the winter's rage
Freeze thy blood less coldly.

In his master's steps he trod
Where the snow lay dinted
Heat was in the very sod
Which the Saint had printed

The story has been Christianised as so many of our old tales are but the truth of what Wenceslas could do is still there ... and he would have done it because he was connected, was walking the deer trods.

The words to the carol "Good King Wenceslas" were written by John Mason Neale and published in 1853, but the music originates in Finland 300 years earlier. Wenceslas himself was the king of Bohemia in the 10th century.

As I mentioned in my book *Elen of the Ways*, my father taught me about what we called foot-dowsing.

When any of us step, walk, run, touch the Earth with our feet, we give out and pick up energy with each step. This happens whether we are conscious of it or not; walking, following the deer trods is partly about becoming conscious of this and about how we do it.

This energy is coloured by how we are because it has passed through us. If we are not connected, but wrapped up in ourselves, our egos, the little self that lives only in this incarnation, then the energy we give out won't be very good. It will be full of our own things and thoughts and feelings, both good and bad, our own fears and selfishness as well as our joys and happiness. But it will all be personal, "about me"; the connection won't be properly made, if it's there at all, because the whole focus will be on "me". Just think for a moment how it feels to you to when you draw in bad energy from wherever you are. We've all done it, most unpleasant. Now think how the Earth feels, and all the trees, plants, rocks, water, fish, animals and birds. And this is what most people give out every day.

When we are connected, beginning with the Earth/Sun exercise, then the energy from Earth and Sun will wash through us and help to clean us up, widen our perspective, take our attention off ourselves and out into everything else. The exercise helps ... but we still have to work on it. It's not like confession where you can sin all week, go to confession on Friday and get cleaned up so you can go out and sin again all the next week! Otherworld certainly does not work like that!

This giving and taking of energy is part of the plan, what the Earth wants us to do; being connected means we can learn to do it properly. Connecting and learning to walk the deer trods helps you give good energy.

As I said in *Elen of the Ways*, feeling, sensing the threads, for me, is like walking on a musical instrument, a big one with many different notes, like harp-strings or organ pipes as they are being played. And it's my walking that plays this great instrument. Dad used to take me out walking from as soon as I could walk, in the park, the grounds of the ruined castle in the town where we lived and out on Dartmoor. He taught me to feel into the land and sense her. At the same time he'd teach me to see the physical signs that told what creatures had been down the path before us, so bringing together spirit and matter. He called it seeing with your feet.

It's the Earth *and* her connection with the Sun that makes it possible for you to see with your feet. Once on that thread it's much easier to connect with the spirit of place of where you are; spirits of place, genius loci, are a sort of step-down from the Earth spirit, smaller and especially concerned with that particular place. Working with the spirit of the place you are in will bring you so much more kenning.

Our long-time ancestors too knew this and were much closer to spirit then than we are now. They followed the deer trods as a normal and natural part of life and living, we have to relearn the old ways; it takes time and lots of practice and patience, but the reward is joy.

Being Useful

As you get to know the deer trods you get to feel yourself to be a part of them, of the spirit which is the Earth herself; you learn to *work with* her, and to *working with* is what our tradition is about. We don't control, command or dominate, we work with. We *ask* Earth and Otherworld – as we call the three worlds that make up our current reality – to show us what they need, *ask* them to show us what we can do to be useful. Being useful is what we want to do, what following the deer trods is about; we don't do it for our own grandeur, but to help the Earth and everything in/on her.

Being useful does help your own development, your personal development, as well. You grow naturally, organically and with the help of everything around you rather than from focusing a personal spotlight on yourself. Focusing on your own development is person-centred, self-centred ... not Earth-centred. Some people think they must know themselves before they can be fit to work for the Earth; they spend years, lifetimes even, trying to perfect themselves so they're "good enough" to work for the Earth. This doesn't actually work! All that time spent on the "self" means that your vision turns inward ... and this can be as painful and useful as an ingrowing toenail!

I need to take you back to making mistakes successfully. Yes, you will make mistakes, but at least you will be learning. It's very likely the Earth will survive your mistakes. She may even be able to put them to good use after all – don't make assumptions this will always be the case though! And your focus will be on *her* needs not your own.

And ... it *isn't* good enough to "have the right intentions"! You do have to do your very best to be appropriate and get it as right as you can. Being sloppy and thoughtless, calling for Otherworld to rescue you every time you get lost, earns you a slap rather than brownie points. You have to work, be observant, do research, and above all *ask* ... ask, ask and ask again. Everyone/thing in Otherworld will respond to your asking (rather than crying for rescue) and give you answers; your job is to learn to see the answers, especially when they don't appear how you expected them to.

- Remember ... be full of expectancy but have no expectations.
- Remember ... the only stupid question is the one you *didn't* ask.

This is how it is when you follow the deer trods.

For us in the British tradition it is important to get our priorities right. Many people in new age work have personal development as their primary goal. As awenyddion, we don't. In the British tradition our primary goal is to help the Earth and in order to do this we learn to ask her what she needs rather than thinking we know best and know what she wants.

This is fundamental ... learning to ask. We'll be doing this more and more through the book. By the end it can be in your bones to ask.

The Earth/Sun exercise helps you learn how to ask. Do it every day, morning and evening. It will soon come to be part of your autopilot and you'll be able to do it really quickly, in fact you'll find you're always *on the thread* so all you have to do is to *touch in* and you're connected. Touching into the thread will enable you to ask what's needed and get the reply pretty well instantaneously.

This is the beginning of following the deer trods.

4

The Three Worlds

In this work the structure of life, the universe and everything is based on the World Tree.

The concept of the World Tree is found in many shamanic traditions including our own. The ancient traditions around the world know the structure of the three worlds and several use the tree as the model for it. You find the three worlds everywhere although the names for them are different depending where you are; each tradition uses names that reflect the land where those people live. If you look deep you'll find they are all fundamentally the same.

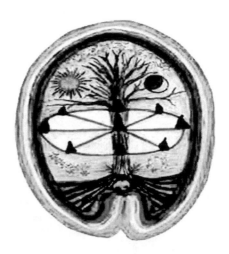

Figure 2: World Tree

In Britain the World Tree is the oak; it grows throughout Britain. This image is of a double-ended tree and comes from an ancient stone roundel found in Derby. It's inscribed with the word *duir*, which means *oak*, and with the name *Darwent* (now Derwent), which is the name of the river that runs through Derby.

Figure 3: World Tree Derby

In the drawing of the Derby oak the roots and branches inter-twine symbolising the interconnection between Lowerworld and Upperworld, the one feeds the other and both feed and are fed by the trunk of Middleworld. Middleworld is where we live and move and have our being. Intercommunication between Lowerworld and Upperworld happens through us as well as through the intertwining roots and branches when we follow the deer trods.

The structure of the three worlds is an integral part of our old ways. Getting to know their structure is very helpful is learning a map, so you have some idea of your way around when you journey there.

The three worlds are …

- **Middleworld** is the place of *love*. It is spirit counterpart of the everyday world we know and live in; it's where things can change and grow.
- **Lowerworld** is the place *wisdom*. It's world of the Ancestors, of everything that ever has been.
- **Upperworld** is the place of *power*, of potential, of every-

thing that will be and can be, of concepts and ideas before they come into manifestation in Middleworld.

Middleworld Energy

The energy of love can be the most enabling thing. Love itself is such a clean and clear thing, it holds no desire to change anything or anyone, but offers choice to everything.

It can be hard for us to appreciate this as very often when we say we love something it actually isn't the thing or person itself that we love, but our own idea of them. As such it's not love, but our desire to change the person/thing into our dream of what we think it should be.

A good test of whether this is happening is to notice if you have used the word *should*, either in your mind or out loud, with regard to this person or thing. Should is a word that needs to be used very sparingly and with great thought, it means that you want to change something or that someone is not conforming to your ideas of rightness.

The word should holds the concepts of *ought to*, *has a duty to*, *is supposed to* … how does it feel to have any of those applied to you?

Love is about seeing clearly, it is enabling, allowing, who or whatever to choose for themselves.

The energy of the Mother holds all of the above. The Mother is about giving life and nourishment, care, protection and, at the same time, the offer of risk. The Mother enables us, but she does not mollycoddle us. The Earth is our Mother, she gives us life, but forces nothing on us.

The healer is not someone who cures or makes things better, nor are they someone who brings things "back to normal" … very far from it! The healer makes things whole.

To make something whole is a very different thing from curing and indeed it can include helping someone to die. The healer knows when to leave well alone as well as when to go in and help. To make whole is what each and every one of us is here to do.

Consciousness is an amazing thing and not many of us use it most of the time! It is both joyful and painful. To be conscious, fully conscious, is to truly experience everything … and some of that experience will be hard, difficult and painful.

Beauty sounds easy. We all love beauty … don't we? But what is beauty? Do we all see it the same way? No, of course we don't.

Beauty as Middleworld energy is about the Earth and what she sees as beauty. Sometimes that can be things like a huge storm, an earthquake, a volcano erupting, a tornado, a tsunami … all things most humans would think of as terrible. This is because we're thinking of it only from our tiny human viewpoint! We rarely want to look beyond our personal viewpoint and we judge everything from this human perspective. We say "It's not fair!" as though the Earth should consider us before she does anything. Of course she doesn't. She does take us into consideration … along with everything else, but our needs are certainly not paramount to her.

Her concept of beauty is the world as a whole, as a complete being. When things get out of balance, often nowadays because of something we humans have thoughtlessly done, then she works to put the balance right. As we're finding out, this can be very uncomfortable for us!

The awenydd works with the Earth to help her put balances right.

Lowerworld Energy

Wisdom is a complex brew of time and space. It's about work, enlightenment, the *Aha!* moment, the seeing of patterns, the bringing together of threads and ideas, of experience, of walking and observing and listening.

It is *not* the same as knowledge! Knowledge is a collection of pictures, ideas, guesses, theories, stories and even the occasional fact, which get stored in one's head or in a book or library. Knowledge is something one can learn … but all that learning may never climax into that incredible brew of knowing and enlightenment.

The Crone is one who has spent and taken the time to experience as much as possible. In the case of the Earth she has experienced everything that has happened to her since she formed, and she remembers it all. She has the accumulated wisdom from everything that has ever happened and she feeds this to the Maiden in Upperworld to feed her creativity.

The Poet is the one who is able to transmit the wisdom in such a way that it can be heard and absorbed by the listeners; a story-teller or, as we say in the British tongue, a cyfarwydd.

The mind is the thing that is able to store and hold this wisdom and produce it on demand – a bit like a hard disc drive.

Truth is another difficult one to comprehend. To know truth means climbing out of one's box and seeing what is really there; as this can be unpleasant in all sorts of ways many people resist doing it. Truth is about losing one's illusions, no longer wearing rose-coloured spectacles, not giving any benefit of doubt, but seeing the truth, however uncomfortable that is.

It's also about being able to see that truth and separate out the feelings of judgement we may have as we know it. Not that the judgement feelings are necessarily wrong, but we mustn't confuse and conflate them with our ideas of truth or we won't see true. We can see that an act is bad, that a person has bad intentions and still love that person even when we see the truth. We can also hate someone when we see the truth. But we don't let our prejudices of either love or hate colour our idea of what is really happening.

Upperworld Energy

When you work with Upperworld you work with *power*, the energy of the *Maiden* and of the *Smith*, the energy of *life* itself.

Power is an energy many people have trouble with. How often do you see people use the words *love and light* as a signature, how often do you see them add the word power? Everyone, every one of us, has worked inappropriately with power in another incarnation. We have an instinctual memory of this and a fear of doing it again so we try to leave the whole idea of power out of our lives altogether. This is cutting ourselves off from one of the three threads of life that we cannot work without. To be without power is to be like a car with no engine … we ain't going nowhere!

It's useful to consider the two basic forms of power …

- Power *over* something/someone.
- Power *to enable* something/someone.

The first one, power over, is disabling and intended to be to aggrandise the one with the power. It is the way of what's become known as the "black magician", out for themselves.

The second is enabling, it gives power and the way to use it is to help someone or something. It is the way of the awenydd.

So working with Upperworld is to learn the difference between these two ways of using power and that can be very subtle.

An example of power over something is the parent who "wants what's best" for their child without ever asking or considering what the child might want and enjoy! That's a tough one to take hold of because I suspect every single one of us has done this to someone at some time. It's not just a parent-thing, wives and husbands will do this to each other, so will friends, employers, and especially governments! Jung used to say to his students, "Never know best and never know first!" It's well worth attempting to live by this; it will help you work with power appropriately.

There are lots more examples of using power inappropriately

27

that I'm sure you'll be able to think of for yourself. The best way to do this is to imagine, "How would I feel if somebody did this to me?" That really works! The ability to put yourself into the shoes (deer trods) of somebody else is really necessary for this work.

Some ideas for the concept of Maiden that will help you get the idea of Upperworld are *original, innovative, creative, primary, prototype, archetype*. The Maiden energy we work with in Upperworld is all of these because it is the place of ideas, new concepts and original archetypes. Remember, Upperworld is the place of *potential*, of everything that will be or can be, of concepts and ideas before they come into manifestation in Middleworld.

The Smith is one of Brighid's three faces. She is the blacksmith, the maker, the forger, the creator, the one who fires and hammers into shape and then quenches the shape in the cold water to fix it. She uses power to create.

Life … life is being, the will to be, the power of being and of enabling others to be.

Good is another difficult one. It's about allowing and enabling again and never knowing best! A useful way of understanding *good* is to come to understand that what is good in one situation, for one person, is not necessarily good in or for another. Let's consider shit. If we keep our shit in our bodies, get constipated, sooner or later it will kill us. If we put shit into the compost heap then the bugs and microscopic life and the fungi all eat it, take it apart and remake it into wonderful food for plants, which are wonderful food for animals and so our own shit comes back to us, but in a form that gives us life rather than taking it. It's worth remembering that human shit works best with trees who can take it in and transmute it into food and so bring it back to Earth.

So, working with the three worlds requires a lot of thought and effort, understanding and a massive opening up of our minds and as well as the growing of consciousness.

Exercise: Earth/Sun

You have already experienced the World Tree through the Earth/Sun exercise. Let's go through it again …

- In the Earth/Sun exercise you begin in the middle … the place where you live, Middleworld.
- From Middleworld you travel downwards into the heart of the Earth, the heart of the Mother where you meet her glowing spark. You twine with that spark and together you travel back up the threads that have grown out of you, your heart, and carried you down into the Mother's heart.
- Then you and the Earth-spark travel up the threads through you and continue out through the top of your head out into space on your way to the Sun. The Sun is the Earth's partner, the Sun enables life. You both arrive at the Sun and all three of you – you, Earth-spark and Sun-spark – twine together and then all three of you travel back down the threads that come from you, through you, back to the heart of the Earth.
- Now, all three of you travel between the heart of the Earth and the heart of the Sun for several moments, getting to know each other, communing together.

It sounds so simple, doesn't it?

Now consider … when you do the Earth/Sun exercise you are doing the work (in little) of the trunk of the World Tree. Communication, energy and life pass up from Mother Earth, through you, to the Sun; Sun energy, life and communication pass down through you to Mother Earth. Sun and Earth communicate, gift and share life through you … and you are enlivened by their sharing along with the rest of the planet and her creatures, plants, rocks and everything.

- What do you suppose happens if (when) you are able to

maintain this connection all the time?

The three worlds carry many energies and correspondences ...

Upperworld	Middleworld	Lowerworld
Power Love	Wisdom	Maiden Mother
Crone	Smith	Healer
Poet Life	Consciousness	Mind
Good	Beauty	Truth

These are by no means all the possible three-ness correspondences, but they give you an idea of what I'm talking about.

5

The Four Elements

The World Tree holds the vertical axis on which the three worlds spin. The vertical axis is like the *warp-threads* in weaving; these are threads on which the pattern is woven.

Middleworld holds the horizontal axis of the four elements. These are the weft-threads that weave the pattern of life.

The four elements – earth, air, fire, water – are the weft-threads.

These two, the warp and the weft, are the basis for the duality which enables life to be.

Imagine the World Tree pulsing with the vertical energy that flows between the Earth and the Sun. This energy pulses up and down, flowing through the tree; you've experienced this in yourself with the Earth/Sun exercise.

The energy also flows out through Middleworld and out into the world itself, feeding and nourishing.

Think of that in terms of the Earth/Sun exercise you do. You enable the energy to flow vertically between Earth and Sun, and horizontally out into the world and back from the world to join again with the vertical flow. So the whole "jolly boiling" (as my mother used to say) gives and takes from each other; without any one the others would die; each takes from the others and each gives to them.

What are these energies that flow out and in through Middleworld?

These are the four elements. I'm not talking about the way science looks at things; that is perfectly valid and very necessary, but in this work we're not talking about the same thing.

The four elements we use in following the deer trods, and in many other traditions, are ...

- Earth
- Air
- Fire
- Water

They correspond to many things and this table gives you an idea of some of them, but it's certainly not a complete list ...

Elements	Earth	Water	Air	Fire
States	Solid	Liquid	Gas	Plasma
Seasons	Winter	Spring	Summer	Autumn
Plants	Roots	Leaves	Flowers	Fruits
Subtle Bodies	Etheric	Astral	Mental	Intuitional
Jung	Sensory	Feeling	Thinking	Intuitive

- Please note, these correspondences are not the same in every tradition; this is because we all work with the spirit of place of where we live.

Let's play with each of the four elements.

Earth

Earth in this sense is not the Earth herself, but the spirit of the fabric of herself, her *body*. Earth is solid; it holds the darkness of the womb of winter; it nourishes the roots of everything; it carries the etheric body, the spirit counterpart of the physical; it holds the sensory sense of touch, which we develop into what we call *body-knowing*.

In the physical, everyday world her body is made of the mineral kingdom that consists of soil, rock, sand, lava, all the stuff that's in the various layers of the Earth's crust and the molten stuff below that at her heart. It's also all the chemical minerals that these contain. And it's the growing medium for all plants that is partly created from the dead bodies of plants, and of animals and humans, which decay and compost down to become soil again.

Every single atom and particle that makes up the Earth has spirit.

Every single atom and particle that makes up our bodies comes from these atoms of the Earth's body. She gives us the materials to make ourselves a spacesuit to house our spirit while we're incarnate here. When we die we give it all back to her again so it can become something else, someone else's spacesuit; it has all been used before we incarnated this time and it will all be used again when we're gone.

The spirit(s) of all this stuff is what we honour and work with when we work.

The spirit of Earth is about containing, holding. It's also about exchange; we exchange the atoms in our bodies every day as well as when we die, most of the dust you clean in your house is dead skin cells. More comes from the food you ingest and later eject, which is more earth molecules … and their spirit counterparts … so, as the old adage says, what goes around comes around.

Water

Water is liquid; it carries the energy of springtime and the energy that makes leaves, one of the major means by which plants feed; it carries the astral body, the body that carries images rather in the way virtual reality does and so enables us to dream and create new ideas; it carries the feelings that enable us to interact with everything around us. It is vital for life, we will not live long without water.

Water is the fluid element that can form and fill any shape.

Water is able to be a solid, a liquid and a gas … ice, water, steam … but not plasma.

There is only so much water on Earth … it moves continually

through its cycle of evaporation, transpiration, condensation, precipitation, and runoff. The runoff usually reaches the sea, most often through rivers and, from there, begins it cycle all over again. Its evaporation and transpiration contribute to the precipitation that we call rain.

We cycle water through our own bodies in a similar way; we breathe out, sweat, collect it within our bodies, pee it out ... which goes down the loo and so, eventually, back into the sea to begin the big cycle all over again. We drink water that has been through each of us, day in and day out.

Water holds memory. It can retain an imprint of energies to which it has been exposed. The theory was first proposed by the late French immunologist Dr Jacques Benveniste, in a controversial article published in 1988 in Nature, as a way of explaining how homeopathy works. Benveniste was pilloried by the scientific community, but in 2013 new research from the Aerospace Institute of the University of Stuttgart in Germany was published that supports the theory that water has a memory.

The human body is made of 60 percent water: the brain, 70 percent; the lungs, nearly 90 percent. Our energies travel in physical form on the flow of water through our bodies ... and into those of other living beings of all kinds.

Water as the fluid element carries the energy. About 70 percent of the planet is covered in water. Again, the energies of everything travel through this magical substance into everything else. It shows us that we are everything and that everything is us; this is a very obvious way of showing us the interconnection of everything. So, again, we see that what goes around comes around.

Air

Like earth and water, air is about the atoms and molecules that make up the physical atmosphere of our planet, and their spirit counterparts. It, too, is part of the Earth's body.

It's also the element that enables sound. Without air there is no sound. There is no sound out in space, despite the special effects of various films! Sound happens when air molecules knock together, collide. When you speak air comes out of your mouth at various speeds (called frequencies in the business) depending on how your vocal cords have manipulated that air. That air then hits the air molecules around you, they hit the next molecule and so on, and so on, until some of them hit somebody's eardrum and make it vibrate (also at frequencies). Those vibrations get translated by your brain into sounds. Of course, the molecules hit your eardrums, too, which is how you hear yourself talking. That's a very simple idea of what happens. Any biologist and physicist will give you a far more detailed explanation.

All of those air molecules and atoms and particles have spirit too. They carry energy and give it to us along with the air we breathe, the sounds we make and receive; everything to do with air. They are part of how we communicate.

Air is the most important thing for life on planet Earth. For us animals it supplies the oxygen that enables breathing and so oxygenates our blood enabling us to live. For plants oxygen is the excreta (shit) that they exhale into the atmosphere as the waste product of photosynthesis, one of the ways they make food for themselves. Plants do photosynthesis by combining carbon dioxide and sunlight with the chlorophyll in their leaves – carbon dioxide is another component of air. There are many more gases in our air all of which are necessary for various of the Earth's purposes; by volume, dry air contains 78.09 percent nitrogen, 20.95 percent oxygen, 0.93 percent argon, 0.039 percent carbon dioxide, and small amounts of other gases including about 1 percent water vapour.

The air, the atmosphere, also protects life on Earth by absorbing ultraviolet solar radiation, warming the surface through heat retention (greenhouse effect), and reducing temperature extremes between day and night. Without these we would not be able to live here.

We breathe in, the air goes through us, then we breathe out. The same happens for every living thing on Earth. There is only so much air here on Earth because there are only so many atoms that make up the Earth (apart from a few meteorites, which make up only a fractional part of the number) so yet again we see that what goes around comes around.

Fire

Fire is plasma. It carries the energies of autumn, the fire of the leaves as the tree prepares to shed them for its winter hibernation and the fire of the harvested fruits that nourish us so well before the coming cold season. It also holds the intuitional and intuitive parts of ourselves, those bits that – when we have learned the skills – help us to work well with Otherworld.

Fire is an incredible substance. In so far as fire is physical, it's actually able to become plasma ... and that *isn't* physical in the same way as earth, air or water.

Plasma is one of the four fundamental states of matter, the others being solid (earth), liquid (water), and gas (air). But plasma is different. Plasma is formed when air or gas is ionized. It is the most abundant form of matter in the universe. Most stars are in a plasma state including our own Sun.

Ionization is weird to the non-initiate non-scientist. It's about atoms or molecules acquiring a negative or positive charge by gaining or losing electrons to form ions. It can happen after collisions with sub atomic particles, collisions with other atoms, molecules and ions, or through the interaction with light. And it can occur through radioactive decay when an excited nucleus transfers its energy to one of the inner-shell electrons causing it to be ejected. Has that blown your mind?

It can also be induced by a strong electromagnetic field, as it is in our Sun. We can see some of the effects of this plasma ball every day; they include heat and light, two things that make life possible.

Unlike water or earth, plasma doesn't have a definite shape or a volume unless it is enclosed in a container, and it has the ability to form structures such as filaments, beams and double layers. All of this makes it very strange stuff. It's probably the closest thing we know (at present) to spirit.

If you want to have fun ionising fire and watching what happens, try this … put a rare earth (Neodymium) magnet on the end of a stick and see how it affects the behaviour of a flame. It's like making your own solar flares with a candle! It happens because the magnet affects the ions and free electrons in motion very strongly.

As a correspondence with the physical realm, fire is about seeds and birth and rebirthing. The old stories of the phoenix are about this. Fire works in and through and sometimes activates seeds, in both plants and animals.

Fire is spirit much more completely and obviously than the other three elements. It helps us understand birth and death and how they are two sides of one coin.

Working with the Elements

When we work with the elements – earth, water, air and fire – we can learn so much from the energy each of them carries. They hold all of our ancestral memories from the very moment our Earth was formed and they go back even before that for all the elements that make up our Earth come from the cosmos. All of those elements have been cycling and recycling forever – since the Big Bang if you hold to that theory, or forever and ever if you prefer the breathing in-and-out theory. We can, every one of us, learn to connect to the elements and ask them to show us more and more of who and what they are. It is huge!

The following exercise will help you begin this lifelong journey.

Exercise: Befriending Your Subtle Bodies

This exercise introduces you to the four elements *within yourself*. It may feel simple, but it is very effective and will help you live your life as well as learning the deer trods ... and/and – this is the British way. I hope you will use it over and over for the rest of your life. It is so useful and helpful and gives you a whole new perspective on the elements and how they work within yourself. It also helps you to know yourself.

You are going to befriend the spirits of the four elements that make up you. They are called the *subtle bodies*.

The four subtle bodies are the ...

- *Sensory body*
- *Feelings/emotions*
- *Thinking*
- *Intuition*

This table will help you make connections and get to know the four elements as well as the subtle bodies. Jung calls them the Four Functions.

Jung	Element	Subtle Body (esoteric name)
Body-sensory-touch	Earth	Etheric
Feelings-emotions	Water	Astral
Thinking-everyday-mind	Air	Mental
Intuition-heart-mind	Fire	Causal

We mostly take our subtle bodies for granted, but each is a spiritual entity in its own right. Each has its own intelligence and knowing and can offer good advice. They all work a lot better when you acknowledge, recognize and befriend them, and consult them about all the things you need to do in order to live your daily life. Nobody thrives on neglect.

This exercise will help you make a good relationship with

your subtle bodies. Try to do it at least once a week, more if you can. As you get more practised you'll find it takes less time and that you can do it in less formal situations because you will have made friends with each of the bodies and so they will work with you easily.

Read the whole process through three times so you begin to have it inside you.

Sort out the space you're going to work in.

You'll need …

Paper
Pencils
Crayons
Tissues
Water
Cushions or chairs

Before you do the exercise, practise moving about in the space so you know how easy or difficult it's going to be and can rectify anything impossible before you actually do the work.

Exercise

Make space on the floor. Get five pieces of paper and write these headings, one per sheet.

- Body/Sensory self
- Thinking self
- Intuitive self
- Feeling self
- Watcher/Observer

Lay the pieces of paper in a cross-pattern, as follows …

- Body *opposite* Intuition

- Thinking *opposite* Feeling
- Observer/Watcher at the centre

Make sure you have plenty of physical space so that you can move to each place easily.

Make a recording of the following instructions to talk yourself through the exercise.

Recording words ...

Sit in the centre, the place of the Self, and clear yourself of worry and thoughts. Just sit there and allow stillness to come.

< 2 MINUTE PAUSE >

Now, move to the place of **Body**. Sense yourself making contact with your Body essence. Ask Body ... *How do you view our life at present?* Ask for an image, word, phrase, or sensation for your life at this time. Spend the next three minutes listening to your Body.

< 3 MINUTE PAUSE >

Soon now it will be time to leave Body and return to your Centre. Thank Body for what it has given you and say you will return to speak with it again. Now, return to your Centre. Make a few brief notes or drawings to remind you of what Body said.

< 2 MINUTE PAUSE>

Spend a moment clearing yourself of the sense of being with Body.

< 1 MINUTE PAUSE >

Now move to the place of **Feelings**. Feel yourself making contact with your Feeling essence. Ask Feelings ... *How do you view our life at present?* Ask for an image, word, phrase or feeling for your life at this time. Spend the next three minutes listening to your Feelings.

< 3 MINUTE PAUSE >

Soon now it will be time to leave Feelings and return to your Centre. Thank your Feelings for what they have given you and say you will return to speak with them again. Now, return to your Centre and make brief notes/drawings.

< 2 MINUTE PAUSE >

Spend a moment clearing yourself of being with Feelings.

< 1 MINUTE PAUSE >

Now move to the place of **Thinking**. Contact your Thinking essence. Ask Thinking ... *How do you view our life at present?* Ask for an image, word, phrase or picture for your life at this time. Spend the next three minutes listening to your Thinking self.

< 3 MINUTE PAUSE >

Soon now it will be time to leave Thinking and return to your Centre. Thank Thinking for what it has given you and say you will return again to listen with your thoughts. Now, return to your Centre and make brief notes/drawings.

< 2 MINUTE PAUSE >

Spend a moment clearing yourself of being with Thinking.

< 1 MINUTE PAUSE >

Now move to the place of **Intuition**. Contact your Intuitive self. Ask Intuition ... *How do you view our life at present?* Ask for an image, word, phrase or idea for your life at this time. Spend the next three minutes listening to your Intuitive self.

< 3 MINUTE PAUSE >

Soon now it will be time to leave your Intuitive self and return to your Centre. Thank your Intuitive self for what it has given you and say that you will return to spend time being with it again. Now, return to your Centre and make brief notes/drawings.

< 2 MINUTE PAUSE >

Spend a moment clearing yourself of being with your Intuitive self.

< 1 MINUTE PAUSE >

Now, spend the next three minutes at your **Centre** allowing the experience to flow gently through you.

< 3 MINUTE PAUSE >

Now, spend a couple of moments preparing to return to the everyday world.

< 2 MINUTE PAUSE >

When you are ready, open your eyes, stretch, breathe deeply and move to somewhere comfortable to sit. Take your pieces of paper with you and review them, synthesising the whole experience. **Draw**, take the pressure off the logical mind and put it into the pattern-forming and pattern-recognition mode – so using *both* halves of the brain.

End Recording.

Once you have done the journey the first time, try to make it a part of your regular routine. The advice you get from each of your subtle bodies is advice from the Otherworldly parts of you. They are the easiest parts of yourself to contact and will have excellent comments, information, guidance and counsel for you.

The more you do it the easier it becomes so you can do it quickly and in everyday consciousness. Clicking in with your subtle bodies every day to ask them to help check out how you are and offer suggestions for your work that day, week, month, year is an excellent practise. I do this exercise a couple of times a week to get a check-up on how I'm doing from Otherworld's perspective, and I *always* do it if there's something stressful happening, it really is helpful.

The more you learn to work readily with Otherworld, like this, the more you will find that following the deer trods becomes a natural process.

6

The Six-Armed Cross

The World Tree contains two axes – the *vertical*, shown through the trunk, and the *horizontal*, shown as the world that spins around the trunk.

The **tree** is the *vertical* axis on which Middleworld, Lowerworld and Upperworld spin. It is the warp on which the pattern is woven.

The **elements** are the *horizontal* axis that spins outwards from Middleworld; they are the weft, the threads that make the pattern.

The three worlds hold the *vertical* dimension, the warp.

The four elements hold the *horizontal* axis, the weft. They weave the pattern of life upon the warp of the tree.

This weaving of the elements is how things come to manifest in Middleworld.

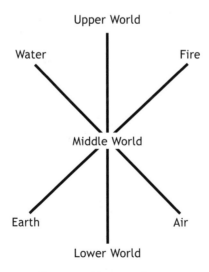

Figure 4: Six-armed cross

We call this diagram the six-armed cross and we use it all the time in this work.

Following the deer trods means you learn to work and weave with the elements of earth, water, air and fire in a similar way to how the goddess, Elen, does it. The elements are the myriad colours of life; they form the shapes and patterns of living through the weaving of the threads and we are some of the weavers. We *all* do this as long as we're alive even if we don't know that we're actually doing it. Every breath you take, everything you do, affects everything else as you saw when we worked through the elements. Following the deer trods is about learning to do this consciously and so constructively and without causing damage.

Before you go any further do this exercise ... it will help you get a real feel for both the three-ness and the four-ness that makes up the six-armed cross. Once you've felt this within your own body you'll gain a far deeper understanding about what it does at other levels ... and it takes the knowledge out of your brain and turns it into wisdom in your body.

Exercise: Being the Six-Armed Cross ...
It's best to be standing up in a place where you are private and alone to do this exercise. You will need enough space around you to extend your arms outwards in any direction.

- Close your eyes and just feel your breath flowing in and out. Don't try to change anything, just allow your breathing to calm you.
- Feel a thread going through you and down into the Earth.
- Feel the thread also going up through you to the Sun.
- Feel yourself on this vertical axis, this thread between Earth and Sun. Feel the energy pulsing from Earth to Sun and Sun to Earth though you. *This is like a quick version of the Earth/Sun exercise.*

- Spend a moment allowing this sense of being on-the-thread to flow through you.
- When you are ready, lift your arms and hold them out at a diagonal from your body, reaching forward and backward out into the space around you.
- Still feel the vertical *down-up* pulse of energy between Earth and Sun flowing through your body, but now add in the *horizontal* pulse of energy flowing from one hand to the other and back again. Feel *both* the vertical *and* the horizontal for a couple of moments.
- When you feel you have this sensation, lower your arms.
- Now raise them again on the opposite diagonal to the one you just held.
- Again, continue to feel the vertical *down-up* pulse of energy between Earth and Sun flowing through your body then, when you feel you have this, add in the horizontal pulse of energy flowing from one hand to the other and back again. Again, feel *both* the vertical *and* horizontal pulses together for a couple of moments.
- When you are ready, lower your arms.
- Let go of the horizontal pulses and thank them for showing you how they are.
- Now let go of the vertical pulses and thank them too for showing you themselves.
- Bring yourself back to the everyday world.
- Make yourself a warm drink.
- Get some paper and coloured pens. Now *doodle* what it felt like for you – don't try to draw, just *doodle*.
- This will help you absorb what you have just experienced so you will – later – come to make more connections and deepen your understanding of it.

What you just did was to *experience* the three vertical and the four horizontal energy directions and how they all meet and flow through you.

Feeling, sensing, gaining *body-knowing* of the six-armed cross and how it is a part of you is essential to the work. Without this body-knowing the three worlds and the four elements will be outside of yourself, external, cut off, and they are not, they are an integral part of you as much as they are of everything else on Planet Earth ... and of the Earth herself.

These are the fundamental threads that weave the pattern of the universe. They work through you as they work through the Earth, the solar system, the galaxies and the universe; and through everything that lives and moves and has its being therein.

Elen brings them to life through her walking of the land, making the deer trods; through her you can come to know them too. Feeling the threads flowing through your own body shows you, in a way no read-lessons can do, what they are about. The old ones always taught us experientially and it works.

As always, don't try to understand what you've just done as yet. Give it space and time; allow it to brew in your cauldron.

7

The Interface

The Interface is a portal between worlds. It's the space where you work with Otherworld. Its shape is the six-armed cross, which is the basis and skeleton for how everything is.

As you come to walk the deer trods knowingly, all the time, you will find that this is where you live; Thomas of Erceldoune, one of our famous awenyddion and better known as Thomas the Rhymer, called it walking between worlds and the phrase has stuck. Like any place where you live you need to do the house-keeping and repairs on it all the time, check every day, do the cleaning, dusting, etc. By working in the Interface every day you do the housekeeping and keep it spick and span, fit for the work you do. You also bring the whole process into your autopilot, into your bones, so that it is always with you and something you work with and refresh all the time.

The Interface is about making sacred space. It is a space *between* the worlds, partly in Otherworld and partly in Thisworld. It opens a *lens-like* space where the two worlds meet and interact. This is where both Otherworld and Thisworld exist in the same space/time. In opening the Interface you create a place where you and Otherworld can meet and work.

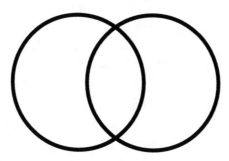

Figure 5: Interface

The six-armed cross is a sphere; you work with it in three dimensions, remember the exercise of Being the Six-Armed Cross? The Interface is the place where the two spheres cross. This space exists because you *and* Otherworld co-operate to make it. Learning how to co-operate, work-with, Otherworld in this sort of creative way is part of what awenyddion do ... they make space where the worlds can meet and exchange energy and ideas very directly.

Figure 6: Reindeer trod

This Interface reminds me of the hoof print of a reindeer. We work in the space between the two toes ...

Working within the Interface has protective qualities too and is far more effective than casting a circle. Its walls are permeable so things can pass through them in both directions; this way you won't trap yourself inside a circle with some nasty thought-form that snuck in when you weren't looking. You can ask anything you don't wish to be there to leave and you can invite anything you do want to come in. You are working with the energy of Elen and her deer trods, and the energy of the World Tree. You create the World Tree, in little, as the space in which you work and you do this *with* Otherworld, not all by yourself. Otherworld are with you every step of the way.

It is an *allowing* rather than a controlling space. It encourages and enables interaction rather protecting from or instilling fear that something might be out there to get you.

This attitude of fear is something of an arrogant and self-absorbed one. Do you really think the beings of Otherworld have nothing better to do than hang around playing tricks on you and making life a misery? Of course not, they are very busy looking after the world, the universe and everything! Humans are only a small (if significant) part of what they do. Evil is made and done and perpetuated by humans ... nothing else does it and especially not Otherworld, despite how the Christians adjusted our old stories to frighten us into submission!

My family, and the old ones in the village where I grew up, taught us to create this space through the World Tree and the Earth/Sun exercise ... and Elen's deer trods.

Opening the Interface

Set up your altar ...

Stone *in the North holding the solid energy for Earth*
Flowers *in the East holding the scented energy for Air*
Candle *in the South holding the plasma energy for Fire*
Water *in the West holding the fluid energy for Water*

To open the Interface you go round *deosil* – the way the Sun goes round – like this ...

Stand at the centre of the space and face North. Breathe deeply in *and* out, quiet yourself. Feel the threads going between the heart of the Earth and the heart of the Sun and the energy pulsing down and up those threads, through you.

Now say aloud – *Spirits of* **Earth**, *I greet you and invite you into this place. Guide me, guard me, keep me in the work I am about to do.*

Stand still. Listen to the silence and sounds around and within you.

When you feel it is time turn to the East, breathe deeply in *and* out, quiet yourself and say aloud – *Spirits of* **Air**, *I greet you and* *invite you into this place. Guide me, guard me, keep me in the work I am about to do.*

Stand still. Listen to the silence and sounds around you and within you.

When you feel it is time turn to the South, breathe deeply in *and* out, quiet yourself and say aloud – *Spirits of* **Fire***, I greet you and invite you into this place. Guide me, guard me, keep me in the work I am about to do.*

Stand still. Listen to the silence and sounds around you and within you.

When you feel it is time turn to the West, breathe deeply in *and* out, quiet yourself and say aloud – *Spirits of* **Water***, I greet you and invite you into this place. Guide me, guard me, keep me in the work I am about to do.*

Stand still. Listen to the silence and sounds around you and within you.

When you feel it is time turn back to the North, breathe deeply in *and* out, quiet yourself, look up to the Sun and say aloud – *Sun Father, I greet you and invite you into this place. Guide me, guard me, keep me in the work I am about to do.*

Stand still. Listen to the silence and sounds around you and within you.

When you feel it is time, breathe deeply in *and* out, quiet yourself, look down towards the heart of the Earth and say aloud – *Earth Mother, I greet you and invite you into this place. Guide me, guard me, keep me in the work I am about to do.*

Stand still. Listen to the silence and sounds around you and within you.

When you feel it is time, breathe deeply in *and* out, quiet yourself, sense inwards to the centre of your own being and say aloud – *I greet you, my own spirit, and acknowledge you within me. Guide me, guard me, keep me in the work I am about to do.*

Stand still. Listen to the silence and sounds around you and within you.

When you feel it is time, breathe deeply in *and* out, quiet yourself and return to everyday space/time.

Let go of the ritual. You are now ready to begin your work or exercise.

Closing the Interface

Close the Interface at the end of the work. This enables you to thank the spirits you've been working with; it also cleans up the space from any bits of yourself and the work you've been doing, leaving it clean for everyone else.

You do this by working in reverse, going *widdershins* through the seven directions, the other way round from opening it, the opposite way round to the way the Sun goes.

Begin at the centre and say – *Thank you, my own Spirit, for guiding, guarding and keeping me in the work I have just done.* Wait, listen …

Look down to the Earth and say – *Thank you, Earth Mother, for guiding, guarding and keeping me in the work I have just done.* Wait, listen …

Look up to the Sun and say – *Thank you, Sun Father, for guiding, guarding and keeping me in the work I have just done.* Wait, listen …

Turn to the West and say – *Thank you, Spirits of Water, for guiding, guarding and keeping me in the work I have just done.* Wait, listen …

Turn to the South and say – *Thank you, Spirits of Fire, for guiding, guarding and keeping me in the work I have just done.* Wait, listen …

Turn to the East and say – *Thank you, Spirits of Air, for guiding, guarding and keeping me in the work I have just done.* Wait, listen …

Turn to the North and say – *Thank you, Spirits of Earth, for guiding, guarding and keeping me in the work I have just done.* Wait, listen …

Stand still. Listen to the silence and sounds around you and within you. When you feel it is time, breathe deeply in *and* out, quiet yourself and return to everyday space/time.

Let go of the ritual. You are now ready to go on with everyday life.

Making Sense ...

There's no need to "make sense" of all this work you've just done, in fact it's a really good idea *not* to try to do so. Instead, give your mental processes a holiday, send them off to the Bahamas and tell them to grow roses! This allows your feelings, your intuition and (most importantly) your body-knowing space and time to work without being harried by your thinking.

We are so heavily encouraged, coerced even, to "think" our way through everything that it's become an unconscious habit for most of us. This is a habit you must let go of in order to follow the deer trods.

The thinking process is seriously bad at working with this kind of thing. It's really rather like Cinderella's ugly sisters cutting bits of toe and heel off their feet so they could attempt to push the bleeding, crippled stumps into the glass slipper and win the prince! Don't do that to yourself; don't try to fit yourself into some kind of "normal" box; that is how to fail completely. In a sense what we do in following the deer trods is allow them – allow the deer trods themselves – *to make sense of us* rather than us trying to "think" them into our safe normal-box ... and that entails keeping the mental processes well out of the picture.

8

The Web of the Trods

Now you've done some work and learned more about the shape and structure of the three worlds and the four elements it's time to get a deeper sense of what they are. The following work and exercises will give you some ideas to get your teeth into.

The Matrix

The six-armed cross is not just a flat pattern on the ground, but the three-dimensional matrix on which all life on Earth is based. It will greatly help your understanding of its three-dimensionality to do the following two exercises.

Each one will take longer than a day to complete as you need *time to process* as well as the time to do them. There is always a brewing, absorbing and digestive process with all of this work ... to get it into your bones. The process is like cooking, it requires time to brew, time for the flavours to combine into a lovely new taste, time for the textures to evolve into deliciousness. Then there's the time for you to absorb all this lovely nourishment and to digest it. You must *not* try to hurry the process, but allow it to work with you. It actually does the work, not you; it acts upon you and helps you grow and change. It's a form of alchemy.

The exercises will sound simple and perhaps even boring! Please do just as I ask you and see what happens for yourself. I grew up with this stuff, have been doing it all my life as well as teaching it since the 1980s. All those years have shown me that when students do what the instructions say they are delighted with the results. This is Otherworld working, not just me. I'm the transmitter, but they create the experience. Go for it.

Exercise 1

Draw the three worlds and four elements diagram for yourself.

This is quite easy, but you'll get more from it if you follow this obvious-sounding process ...

Draw the vertical axis first.

Put the three worlds on it.

Sit with it for a while and allow images, words and phrases to come into your mind; make a note of these on a separate piece of paper.

Now put the horizontal axes on – earth opposite fire, air opposite water.

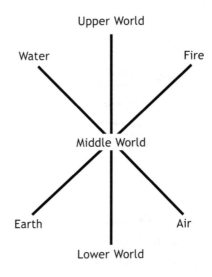

Figure 7: Six-armed cross annotated

Again, sit with them and allow images, words and phrases to come into your mind; make a note of these too on another piece of paper.

Now put the whole thing away and go do something else. This allows the work you've done to brew in your cauldron without you continually worrying at it like a terrier with a bone!

Tomorrow, take the whole caboodle, all three pieces of paper, out again and sit with them (and a cup of tea); make it a time of greeting for today and thanks for yesterday. Let your drawing itself and the three worlds show you more stuff about themselves and how they are all interconnected. You'll be surprised and delighted at what comes to gift itself to you.

Exercise 2

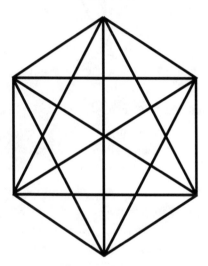

Figure 8: Matrix

This is the three-dimensional matrix. You're going to draw it ...

The drawing process goes like this ...

First you draw the six-armed cross again. Do NOT use the diagram you already did, draw another one. Put the three worlds and four elements on it.

Sit with it for a while.

Go into the sit with *full of expectancy, but with no expectations*! Allow images, words and phrases to come into your mind; make a note of these on a separate piece of paper.

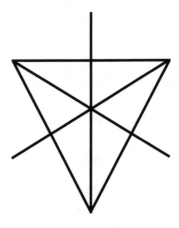

Figure 9: Six-armed cross annotated

Next, join up the points of water and fire with Upperworld, so you have a downward-pointing triangle.

Sit with this diagram and allow it to show you more of itself. Listen how fire and water work together and with the Lowerworld. Allow images, words and phrases to come into your mind; make a note of these on a separate piece of paper.

Put it all away until tomorrow, allow what has come to you to brew, peacefully and undisturbed by your mind and thinking process, in your cauldron.

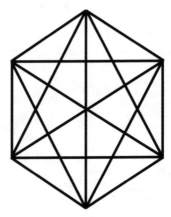

Figure 10: Matrix 1

Next day, take out the whole caboodle of yesterday and sit with for a moment in greeting and thanks for yesterday. When you have greeted your drawing do the next step. This is to connect up the earth and air points with the Upperworld.

Now you have an upward-pointing triangle on top of the downward one.

Figure 11: Matrix 2

Sit with your new configuration and allow it to show and tell you about itself. Let the images, words and phrases come into your mind and make a note of them on another piece of paper.

Then put the whole bundle away again until tomorrow.

Next day, take everything out and sit with it all, greet it and thank it for the past work you've done together. When the bundle has had its interaction with you, including today's images, words and phrases, take the drawing with the downwards and upwards triangles and connect up all the outside points.

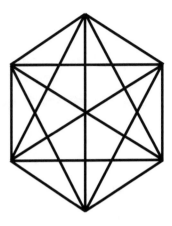

Figure 12: Matrix 3

As you go from point to point do it slowly, name each point as you come to it including the first one from which you begin.

Some people choose to begin in Lowerworld … if this is your choice, ponder on what made you choose to begin here.

Others begin at Upperworld; again, if this is you, ponder and sit with what makes you begin here before you continue on.

Others again choose to begin with the element of earth; sit with this and consider how this comes to be your choice, what it is that pulls you here.

The same goes should you decide to begin at water, fire or air.

When all the points are connected and you have spent time with each of them on the journey round the circumference, sit with the whole diagram and allow it to speak with you. Then put the whole of your work away together in a bundle and leave it alone to brew quietly.

Now you've drawn it, it would be extremely good if you would make a 3D model of it using drinking straws, this would give you a real concept of it.

When you've done this sit with it for a while, just feel into it and allow it to spin its threads into you.

9

Journeying

You've done lots of exercises as you've worked through the book, all of these will have helped to practice you for one of the main pieces of business of being awenydd and following the deer trods … journeying.

Journeying is not the same as meditation; it does have a lot of similarity with what Jung called *active imagination*. Jung was an amazing person, he began his journey into psychology through séances with his cousin and always had a familiar spirit called Philemon. He was, perhaps, the only psychologist who understood in his bones what the word signifies; psyche is Greek for soul, Jung knew this and worked with it.

So what is journeying?

Journeying is making a shift of consciousness.

It is about *going out* into Otherworld and *returning* with something useful for your people.

This is vital to understand … you go out and you return; you go out and come back … as Bilbo said *"there and back again"*. This is what the spirit keeper does.

- The spirit keeper **goes out.**
- The spirit keeper **comes back.**

The fundamental principle of journeying is to go out and to return. For many, indeed all of us at times, it's the return bit that is so hard! But without the return the whole trip is pointless, just a jaunt for personal pleasure that has no giving, no exchange, and so does nobody (even yourself) any good at all.

The awenydd, the spirit keeper, journeys to find wisdom and to bring it back to their people. This is *service* and the root of the spirit keeper's purpose, the root of following the deer trods.

It is easy for most people to trip out, space out ... there are many terms for it ... but the return is often far more difficult. It's so tempting to stay, so easy to get lost out there. Tales of out-of-body and near-death experiences often say how hard it is for the person to return to the everyday world; journeying can be like that too.

It can also be very difficult for the person to bring back the goods, the wisdom s/he has found. The old fairy story of the young person who travels off to fairyland, meets with the fairy queen and is given a gift of gold to take back to his family, is one of the ways this grammarye is told in the British tradition.

The young man wanders into fairyland and finds his way to the castle of the fairy queen. She takes him in, tells him lots of things and, in some versions of the story, he sleeps with her. In the morning she gives him a bag of gold to take back to his family. She tells him to guard it well and be careful to follow her advice when crossing back into his everyday world. He is young and brash and over-confident, he trips lightly back over the border, completely forgetting or taking no notice of the fairy queen's advice, and turns up at his home again. There, he tells his story and, at the end, he produces the bag and empties it onto the table, hoping to astonish his family and become a person of consequence in their eyes. What rolls out of the bag is just stones. No gold. He hasn't followed the fairy queen's instructions. In consequence he looks a fool and is laughed at by his family.

He tries, sometimes for years, to find his way back to fairyland to get the gold. His journeying is painful and his adventures force him to learn a lot, most especially to ask, he becomes a much humbler and more pleasant person. One day he finds himself in a place that looks familiar. He goes to follow the half-remembered path and then he stops. He asks if this is his path to fairyland. The answer comes back, yes. He follows the path and comes at last to the castle of the fairy queen. Again she invites him in. This time he is far more observant and listens well. In the morning the queen again gives him gold and tells him how to cross the border back to his own world. This time he listens.

He comes to the border and there is an old one sat by the side of the road, as there was the first time. The old one asks him for a gift, a drink of water, and the young man gives the old one the very last drops in his flask. The old one blesses him and sets him on his way to take the right road to cross the border. When he arrives home again his family have all thought him dead these many years, they welcome him. Instead of bragging about his travels he carefully opens his bag and takes out the gold. It is still gold. He tells his family that this is a gift for them, to help them live. He lives there for the rest of his life and becomes one who helps the young people and teaches them wisdom.

Do you get the points in that story? Asking and listening, not bragging or looking to score points, not competing, not trying to be the smartest, cleverest person, but thinking of others before yourself, giving gifts even to your own possible detriment ... all these are the ways of following the deer trods.

Always, the awenydd, the spirit keeper, goes out *and comes back*, bringing the goodness back for the people.

Journey Horse

Many spirit keepers use some form of hypnotic rhythm to catch hold of the everyday mind and send it to sleep while the spirit goes out to work. This rhythm is often called the spirit horse. The horse keeps you on track on your journey and reminds you to return.

The most usual form for the horse is drumming; there are lots of drumming CDs around if you want to find and use one. Other forms of sound-rhythm that are good to use are the sound of waves on a beach, the sound of rain, or of a stream or river, so journeying outside can be done easily once you realise this. Some people find the steady roaring of the wind will be the horse that carries them out on their journey. The sound of a hive of bees is a good journey-horse too. I sometimes use a recording of my cats purring and occasionally they are kind enough to do live purring for me. There are many ways so spend some time finding what *you* like to work with.

Exercise: Sacred Space

Use this exercise to practice with. It's good to do this exercise several times as this affirms your sacred space to you. It will also help you *know* your sacred space. You may already have such a place, but this exercise will help you deepen you relationship with it, enable you to be intimate with your sacred space so it becomes somewhere you know in your bones.

You will need ...

A physical space to journey in; it should be somewhere you won't be disturbed for up to 1 hour and where you can lie down comfortably. You will also need:

Water to drink
Notebook and pen
Tissues
Blanket to lie under
Cushions/mat to lie on
Scarf to cover your eyes if you like that sort of thing

Turn off your phone and explain to anyone you live with that you are not to be disturbed.

Now ...

Lie down and settle yourself comfortably.

Do the Earth-Sun connection – you can do this lying down just as well as standing up.

State your purpose, say aloud ... *I ask for a short and simple journey across the worlds, there and back again, to learn how to go out and return and to meet my sacred space. Help me to do this and to return.*

Quiet your mind and allow the journey-horse to carry you across the worlds.

Follow the journey …

Be observant. Note the markers that you pass – gates, stones, bridges, particular trees, whatever you see. This is important, you need to have this sort of observation ability as part of your autopilot; you will use it to help you return.

Find yourself in your special place, your sacred space.

You'll recognise it … even if you've never been there before.

Explore the place, really get to know it, make friends with it, befriend its spirit.

When you feel really at home it'll be time to go back.

Return the way you came – this is important – and note again all the markers you noticed on your outward journey, this is an important part of learning to orient yourself when journeying in Otherworld (and in Thisworld too!).

When you are back, lie still, don't move or open your eyes for a little while, get used to being home, get used to the feel of wearing your body again and thank your body for being there for you to come back to. Know yourself to be returned to your everyday self.

When you are ready, get up and thank your space.

Have a drink of water. Make notes about what happened.

Tidy your space – it's important to clear the space of the work you just did, don't leave old journey-cobwebs hanging around to get dusty and dirty!

Now go and make yourself a hot drink and have something to eat. You've done a lot of work (even if you don't realise this yet) and need to replenish the energy you've expended.

Journeying

You actually did a short journey when you did the exercise above.

What did you bring home with you?

Hopefully a deeper and more intimate knowing of your sacred space; a greater skill in observation; a confidence in yourself that you *can* come back when you go out; possibly some gift and/or new idea from your sacred space; you may even have met and spoken with someone there.

It's easy to get stuck in concepts (boxes) of what we should bring back and these are often quite inappropriate things. All of that knowing I listed above is really useful stuff; it will make you better at following the deer trods, more useful to Otherworld and to those around you. It will also make you know yourself better – this is always good.

You will have noticed that I asked you to say your purpose out loud.

Having a purpose is important for journeying; it's not something to do in the manner of a Sunday afternoon drive to fill in time. Awenyddion don't go tripping off for the fun of it. Such an attitude is dangerous and … it's grossly impolite to do so. How would you feel if a load of day-trippers galumphed about in your garden without even a by-your-leave? Pretty cross, I'd imagine, well so does Otherworld when we treat it with so little respect. Cross folk are quite likely to kick ass … and Otherworldly ass-kicking is uncomfortable to say the least, especially if well deserved!

So awenyddion prepare carefully for each journey, they make sure they know what they are going for and why … and if they should be doing the journey at all. We always need to ask if what we are considering doing is actually the appropriate thing to do; if it isn't then we don't do it.

Preparation and Follow-Up Ritual

This is a very good way to ensure that you only go journeying when you should be and for what you should be.

We use the time of twilight. Twilight is the magic time between the worlds, between the two lights. The word *twilight* is a contraction of the words *two lights*. The two lights are the Sun and the Moon. It is the time when both darkness and light exist together and neither holds sway over the other; it is a time when Otherworldly beings can be seen and heard by those willing to be still enough to ask and listen.

Twilight is also Elen's special time. One of her titles is lady of the twilight, of the two lights. Having done the Earth/Sun exercise this likely makes sense to you now.

Preparation Exercise

Read the exercise through several times and collect together everything you'll need well before you want to begin your three-day ritual. Doing this ahead of time allows the whole process to brew inside you, inside your cauldron, and to begin to be absorbed and digested. Always, always, spend and give time to Otherworldly work. I use those words, *spend* and *give*, very deliberately. All work with Otherworld is about exchange; if you are not willing to spend and give with them they won't spend and give to you.

Do this ritual for three days, at both morning and evening *twilight* or as near to this as you can.

- **Earth**: Take a pinch of earth from your own garden, window box or plant pot. Thank the earth-soil for being there, smooth it gently on your face and leave it there until the ritual is completed.
- **Water**: Hold a glass, or small bowl, of water in your hands. Thank it for being there and sip from it. Keep the rest of the water for the ending of the ritual.
- **Air**: Light a small piece of incense, smell it, watch the smoke rising into the air. Thank it for being there.

- **Fire**: Light a candle. Look into the heart of the flame and thank it for being there.
- **State your purpose**: *"I would like to meet the World Tree. Please tell me how and when and if to do this."*
- **Sit-with** the purpose of your journey. Ask if the purpose is appropriate. Ask if the timing of the journey is appropriate. Ask if you should be doing this journey at all.
- **Listen** to the answers you get. Ask more questions for further clarity as you need. Remember ... the only stupid question is the one you didn't ask!
- **Thank Otherworld** when you have the information you need and end the ritual.
- **Ending**: Wash the earth from your face with the water from the glass or bowl. Rub your hands dry in the smoke of the incense and then douse the incense. Blow out the flame of the candle and as you do so watch the smoke disappear and let it carry these words, aloud, into Otherworld: *"Thank you for guiding me in this"*.

Have something to drink and a snack to nibble.

After doing your ritual, each time, make sure you clean up the space and don't leave physical bits of it scattered about, like the ash from incense, candle wax, spilt water. All these physical things will hold spirit-clutter too; you will *not* have finished your ritual, but still have bits of it clinging to you like old cobwebs. If you do this then you go through the rest of the day wiping bits of old spirit-cobweb onto everyone you pass without even knowing you've done so. This is being unaware and so is bad etiquette! Those who follow the deer trods do their best to be aware! Always clean up after yourself physically and spiritually, don't be a slob.

Journey to the World Tree

Make sure you have everything you need and have cleaned and

prepared your space.

You will need ...

Stone – symbolising earth

Flowers – symbolising air (you can use incense, but I love using fresh flowers)

Candle – symbolising fire

Water – symbolising water

You will also need ...

Tissues

Water to drink

Cushions/mat to lie on

Blanket to cover yourself

Scarf to cover your eyes – if you like that

Notebook and pen, coloured pencils/crayons/pens

Recording of drumming or rhythmic sound to ride on

Ear phones to hear it through

Tell your family and friends that you're not available for at least an hour.

Turn your phone off.

This journey will begin to teach you how to travel between the worlds and bring the wisdom back.

Read the journey-script through three times on days before you do the actual journey, make sure you know your purpose ... then go for it.

- Open the Interface.
- Lie down. Cover your eyes. Put your earphones in.
- Turn the journey-horse recording on.
- Say your purpose out loud, three times: *"I am here to meet the World Tree. I ask Otherworld to help me in this task."*

- Now, lie still. Feel your breathing. Don't try to change anything. Feel yourself lying comfortably and safely under your blanket. Hear the drumming-horse. Allow the *horse* to carry you across the worlds.
- Find yourself in your sacred space. Spend a moment there greeting it, remembering it.
- When you are ready, go to the door/gate that will take you out into Otherworld. Whisper your purpose again to the door/gate and, when you are ready, go out and begin your journey.
- Find yourself beside the World Tree, ask to enter.
- The World Tree may ask you for a gift. If so, there will be one nearby, find it, bring and offer it. World Tree will then grant your entry. Do *not* make assumptions about the gift, ask and check that it's the right one with World Tree.
- Spend time with World Tree; listen, ask your own questions, watch, learn. Some of the time will likely be spent in just being.
- Stay with World Tree. Do NOT be tempted to gallivant off! You may well be tested in this so don't fall into the traps. This is a very important part of your learning, to stay on target, stick to your purpose, not to go off-piste and lose your focus, not to get lost and need to be rescued, not to lose your gold and make a general cock-up of the whole process!
- When the journey is done World Tree will ask for your name. Answer spontaneously from your heart. The answer you give may surprise you. It may, or may not, be your given name or any other you have called yourself by in this lifetime. Allow your heart to direct your voice to say what is needed. Listen to and hear your name, this will be how Otherworld calls you.
- World Tree will give you a gift, accept it with thanks.
- Thank World Tree for *containing* you on your adventure.

- Return to your sacred space. Spend a few moments there pondering your journey.
- Find yourself in Thisworld, lying under your blanket again.
- Don't get up immediately. Turn on one side and curl up in the foetal position for a few minutes. Gently recall, in your mind's eye, where you have been, who you have met, what gifts you have given and received. This is about bringing home the goods from your journey, you need to tell what you have done, seen, given and got over to yourself so that you remember it when you return to being fully awake in Thisworld.
- You are also reclaiming your body, getting to know and feel it again after you have been journeying out of it for half an hour. You need to greet your body and thank it for still being there for you to come back to – don't take it for granted!
- When you are ready, gently sit up, then get up.
- Make any notes you want to.
- Close the Interface.
- Eat and drink to replace the physical energy you have used and to anchor yourself in your body again.
- Don't forget to clear your physical space.

Follow-up after the journey ...

Do this same ritual each morning and evening twilight for the three days *after* the journey:

- **Earth**: Take a pinch of earth from your own garden, window box or plant pot. Thank the earth-soil for being there, smooth it gently on your face and leave it there until the ritual is completed.
- **Water**: Hold a glass, or small bowl, of water in your hands. Thank it for being there and sip from it. Keep the rest of

the water for the ending of the ritual.

- **Air**: Light a small piece of incense, smell it, watch the smoke rising into the air. Thank it for being there.
- **Fire**: Light a candle. Look into the heart of the flame and thank it for being there.
- **State your thanks**: *"Thank you, World Tree, for meeting me. I will visit and learn from you again."*
- **Sit-with** the memory of your journey. Go over it again in your heart; note the things that come to your mind's eye now, after the journey. ·
- **Ask for clarification** whenever you notice yourself wondering about anything as you remember.
- **Thank Otherworld** when you sense that the memories and insights are over for today and end the ritual.
- **Ending**: Wash the earth from your face with the water from the glass or bowl. Rub your hands dry in the smoke of the incense and then douse the incense. Blow out the flame of the candle and as you do so watch the smoke disappear and let it carry these words, aloud, into Otherworld: *"Thank you for my journey"*.

Have something to drink and a snack to nibble.
Don't forget to clean up after yourself as usual!

This is a period of digestion, absorption and gestation so silence is the watch-word. Do *not* tell your experience abroad to all your friends but hold it sacred and secret within yourself or else you will abort it or give it premature birth.

10

Familiar Spirits

When walking the deer trods it's really good to have a companion, one who knows the paths far better than you and who will be there to help you in both work and play, the fun and the scary bits, the delight and despondency ... all the things that will happen along the path.

What is a Familiar Spirit?

Your familiar is your friend, guardian, playmate and helper. They know their way around in Otherworld so ask and listen to them; they will help you find your way there and to make friends with locals.

Elen, the deer lady, deer goddess, is Lady of the Animals. Your familiar knows and loves her deeply so she or he will be well able help and guide you in following the deer trods for they are Elen's ways.

Familiars are companions who walk the deer trods with you. They know the ways, the paths, the silver threads, much better than you as they don't suffer the memory loss most of us get as soon as we are born. This memory loss is vital for our learning and growth; if we came into incarnation with a full memory most of us wouldn't bother to learn anything new and this would be a loss for Otherworld as well as ourselves. Each incarnation is about re-membering – putting together the members (i.e. the limbs of your knowing) again, remaking it deeper and wider than before. Familiars help you do this.

Familiars are our elder brethren, friends who have walked the deer trods longer than we and can help show us the way. They may also guard you when you need it and they will loan you (*loan* not give) their power when you show them you are able to use it appropriately. They are far more than keepers of your power, in fact they don't do this unless you somehow mislay your power.

In other cultures familiar spirits are known as power animals. In the British tradition they are familiars or familiar spirits.

Often the first thing that comes to mind with the word familiar is a picture of a bent old woman, stirring her cauldron, with her black cat sat beside her. While cats do have the knack of being very good at the job they are by no means the only animals who do this – indeed any animal can. The image of the witch and her cat has become demonised along with wolves and crows, wizards and other wise men and women – the cunning folk of my own family for instance.

Familiars are Otherworldly beings who live and work with us. They may also be incarnate and so be present in *both* physical and non-physical space. You may find that, as well as your Otherworldly familiar, you are befriended by one in this world too. They may both be of the same species, or they may be different. If you can take on caring for your physical friend as well this will be very good; if you're worried about it then ask your Otherworldly and your physical familiars to help you find a way. It's perfectly OK to have familiars in Thisworld as well as in Otherworld and they won't be jealous of each other.

That is how it is, being a spirit keeper and one who walks Elen's ways. You are offered a job so you ask for help to take it on. Your first thought in all your actions will change from focusing on yourself first to focusing on the job first.

You may already have a familiar but it *still* good to do this journey to meet them at a new level of intimacy. You may also find that another animal chooses to work with you as well. There is no disloyalty in this. The school concept of *bestest*-friend just does not apply in working with Otherworld; that is a child's concept along with the jealousy and fear of being left out that promotes it. Otherworldly beings are not children, they are ancient, ancient in ways it can be hard to get your head around at first.

Your familiar is *never* yours in the sense of ownership: it's important to realise that you don't own your familiar ... if anything it's the other way around!

- And ... you don't choose your familiar, your familiar chooses you.

The act of being chosen is very sacred. You are chosen by an Otherworldly spirit who wishes to befriend, love, help, play and work with you. You may have worked together before and your familiar will remember this even if you don't. They are also your elder! Do be willing to listen to and learn from your elders, they are happy to teach you but you have to *ask* them to do so and be willing to listen.

Ask! *Asking is the key* to all this work.

- The only stupid question is the one you *didn't* ask!

In order to work with your familiar you need to get to know her or him. Please don't call them "it" – they are not objects but beings in their own right and it is important that your relationship comes from a place of mutual respect.

Living with Your Familiar

Familiars are for life ... there is no divorce! There are no short-term contracts, get-out clauses, terms of reference or any of the other stuff we control freaks like to fence our lives about with, not in Otherworldly work. On the other hand, your Otherworld family will never deceive you; trust is really possible and very necessary across the worlds.

You and your familiar will be working and living together for the rest of your life.

For this to work, you must *build* your relationship with your familiar. It's like making bread, it tastes best when made new every day. Take care of your familiar in this world. Don't neglect them. Work with them every day, while you do the washing up as well as when you're doing magic, develop an intimacy with them.

You will never be lonely, your best friend will always be there for you to call on; they will help you in ways no human can. You will always have a companion to walk beside you on the path, sharing your joys and sorrows, always there for you. It is the most wonderful thing imaginable.

Journey to Meet Your Familiar

Do the same preparation ritual you did before meeting with World Tree for three days before your journey, at both morning and evening *twilight* or as near to this as you can.

This time you have a different purpose; this is about meeting your familiar.

Use these words ...

I am preparing the way to meet a friend
Long have we been apart.
I invite you in
To live with me, to share my days, to watch my ways.
I offer you all that I know.
I will care for you and guard you here in Middleworld.
I ask that you care for me,
Guide me, guard me, keep me, when we walk between the worlds.
Old friend, I call you now.
I will meet with you at the appointed time.
Choose me, come to me, speak to me,
When I enter your realm.

At the ending of this preparation ritual, as you blow out the candle and watch the smoke flow into Otherworld, let the smoke carry these words, aloud, to your familiar ... *"We will be together soon"*.

Journey to Meet Your Familiar

Make sure you have everything you need and have cleaned and prepared your space.

Make sure you have the following ...

Stone – symbolising earth
Flowers – symbolising air
Candle – symbolising fire
Water – symbolising water

Tissues
Water to drink
Cushions/mat to lie on
Blanket to cover yourself
Scarf to cover your eyes, if you like this
Notebook and pen, coloured pencils/crayons/pens
Recording of drumming or rhythmic sound to ride on
Earphones to hear it through

Tell family and friends you're not available for at least an hour and turn off your phone.

Read the journey-script through three times before you do the actual journey, make sure you know your purpose, then go for it.

- Open the Interface.
- Lie down. Cover your eyes.
- Say your purpose out loud, three times: *"I am here to meet my familiar. I ask Otherworld to help me in this task."*
- Now, lie still. Feel your breathing. Don't try to change anything. Feel yourself lying comfortably and safely under

your blanket. Hear the drumming-horse.

- Settle yourself.
- Quiet your mind; allow the *horse* to carry you across the worlds.
- Find yourself in your sacred space. Spend a moment there greeting it, remembering it. Go to the door/gate that will take you out into Otherworld. Whisper your purpose again to the door/gate and, when you are ready, go out and begin your journey.
- Find yourself beside the World Tree.
- Tell World Tree that you are here to meet your familiar and ask World Tree to help.
- The World Tree may ask you for a gift. If so, there will be one nearby, find it, bring and offer it.
- World Tree will tell you what to do next, follow the instructions. This may well mean that you go down to Lowerworld. Lowerworld is the place of the ancestors and your familiar is one of them.
- When you feel you have got to wherever it is you are going to meet your familiar stop still, ASK your familiar to come and choose you.
- You may find yourself in a large group of creatures. Be still and don't be scared. They are watching you, looking at you, seeing what you will do and checking if you are a polite person.
- One or more creatures will come forward – ask each in turn: *"Are you my familiar?"* Ask them three times!
- They will tell you true on the third answer and the one who wishes to work with you will tell you yes. This is a test, can you wait; can you be patient; have you the nous to ask three times? So stand still, ask and wait … it's well worth it.
- Asking three times is a sort of law of Otherworldly physics, whoever it is will tell you true on the third asking. It doesn't work too well with humans in Thisworld though!

- When you are chosen by your familiar go with them; spend and give time with them, listen and watch, learn. Some of the time will likely be spent in just being.
- When it's time (you'll know), ask your familiar to come home with you. They cannot do this without your invitation and they've been waiting all your life for this moment, don't disappoint them.
- Return to World Tree together.
- Thank World Tree for containing your journey.
- When you are both ready, return to your sacred space. Spend a few moments there together, pondering your journey.
- Find yourself in Thisworld, lying under your blanket again with your familiar … know they are there with you even if you can't see them physically.
- Don't get up immediately. Turn on one side and curl up in the foetal position for a few minutes. Gently recall, in your mind's eye, where you have been and what you have done. This is part of bringing home the goods from your journey, you need to tell over to yourself what you have done, seen, given and got so that you remember it when you return to fully awake in Thisworld.
- You are also reclaiming your body, getting to know and feel it again after you have been journeying out of it for half an hour. You need to greet your body and thank it for still being there for you to come back to – don't take it for granted!
- When you are ready, gently sit up, then get up.
- Make any notes you want to. Drawings of your familiar are good to do now too, even if you think yourself a crumby artist!
- Close the Interface.
- Eat and drink to replace the physical energy you have used and to anchor yourself in your body again, and clear

your space. Be aware of your familiar even while you do apparently mundane things like eating and drinking.

- You may find that your familiar would like some special place for them to be in your home; it may be just a cushion or special cloth or throw. It may well be quite an ordinary-seeming place. One of mine enjoys a corner of my sock drawer while another like the top of one of the bookcases!
- Make any notes you want to.
- Eat and drink to replace the physical energy you have used and to anchor yourself in your body again.
- Don't forget to clear your physical space.

Follow-up after the Journey ...

Do this same ritual you did for meeting World Tree each morning and evening twilight for the three days *after* the journey. And use the time to **sit-with** your familiar and deepen your relationship. Go over it again with them and ask them about things that occurred.

And don't forget to have something to drink and a snack to nibble after the ritual. Your familiar may like you to put something out for them too – ask and see.

Don't forget to clean up after yourself as usual!

This is a period of digestion, absorption and gestation so silence is the watch-word. Do *not* tell your experience abroad to all your friends but hold it sacred and secret within yourself or else you will abort it or give it premature birth.

11

Teachers

As well as our familiar spirits we also have teachers who help us follow the deer trods.

Teachers are different to familiars. They may be spirits, they may also have been, or still be, incarnate as humans or not. They may be friendly or they might be quite cool and somewhat aloof. They are teachers rather than friends and have many students to work with not just you.

Teachers are *tricksters*, they help us grow. Tricksters are the very best teachers in all the worlds. They riddle and trick us; tell us part of the story but not the whole; offer us alluring ideas that will lead us up the garden path; they often pander to our current prejudices in order to help us find our own way out of them; they play jokes, make mischief, mislead us, hoodwink us, send us to the shop for a tin of striped paint ...

And I said this is good ... ? Yes, it is.

Humans are far worse than cats about change! You never learn anything if you carry on with the same old expectations and convictions. We huddle desperately in our old boxes, full of old shit and cobwebs and dust and rubbish and baggage that is falling to pieces; we scream rape and murder if someone tries to lift the box-lid let alone help us out of it. And all this old stuff is way past its sell-by date. We can't learn new stuff if we refuse to let go of the old.

Tricksters, teachers, help us to let go and make space for the new. They all keep you on your toes, keep you awake and aware ...

They appear in all sorts of forms, often ones that surprise you; they may be human-ish looking, but maybe not. One student once had a teacher who came as a Klingon, it was a marvellous relationship! Gwydion is the master enchanter of Britain and a well-known and excellent trickster. Fox is the chief British trickster-animal.

All of these are teachers though, *not* familiars, even if they turn up in animal-guise.

Journey to Meet Your Teacher

Do the preparation ritual for three days before your journey, at both morning and evening *twilight* or as near to this as you can. Your purpose for this journey is: "*I go to meet the teacher*".

Ending – as you watch the smoke flow into Otherworld, let it carry these words, aloud: "*I go to meet my teacher*".

Make sure you have everything you need and have prepared and cleaned your space.

Make sure you have the following …

Stone – symbolising earth
Flowers – symbolising air
Candle – symbolising fire
Water – symbolising water

Tissues
Water to drink
Cushions/mat to lie on
Blanket to cover yourself
Scarf to cover your eyes, if you like this
Notebook and pen, coloured pencils/crayons/pens
Recording of drumming or rhythmic sound to ride on
Earphones to hear it through
Tell family and friends you're not available for at least an hour
Turn your phone off or set it to silent

Journey to Meet Your Teacher

Read the journey-script through three times before you do the actual journey, make sure you know your intention then go for it.

- *IMPORTANT* ... Ask your familiar to accompany you on this journey. Never go anywhere without your familiar now.
- Open the Interface.
- Lie down. Cover your eyes.
- Say your purpose out loud, three times: *"I go to meet my teacher"*.
- Settle yourself, lie still. Feel your breathing. Don't try to change anything. Feel yourself lying comfortably and safely, *with your familiar*, under your blanket. Hear the drumming-horse.
- Allow the *horse* to carry you across the worlds.
- Find yourselves, you and your familiar, in your sacred space. Spend and give a little time there greeting and remembering. When you are both ready go out ...
- Find yourself beside the World Tree.
- Say: *"I go to meet my teacher,"* and ask World Tree to help you.
- World Tree may ask you for a gift. If so, there will be one nearby, find it, bring and offer it.
- World Tree will help you go where you will meet your teacher. It's quite likely you will enter the trunk and go up into Upperworld to do this. Upperworld is the place of potential, ideas, and where your teacher spends a lot of time.
- Find your way wherever it is you are to go. When you arrive there may be someone waiting, but maybe not ... don't have preconceptions! Note everything you see, don't be in a hurry.
- Say your purpose aloud, *again*, three times: *"I am here to meet the teacher"*.
- Something will *happen ... Your teacher will come to you.*

- Ask – it's your responsibility to speak first! – ask if they are your teacher. And ask three times! They will be hoping that you now have this knowing in your bones. If you forget they will lead you a merry dance!
- They may not appear as you expect – remember, be full of expectancy but have no expectations.
- Listen ... a lot! And *always* ask questions when you don't understand something.
- Your teacher may take you somewhere, show and tell you things. Whatever it is, go and do it. If you feel uncertain at any time say so and ask them to help you. They will ... but you have to ask!
- If they give you a gift, accept it.
- You may also want to give them a gift; if you don't already have one there will be one near you, find it and gift it.
- You will know when it is time to leave ... *make sure your familiar is with you* and don't get lost!
- Thank World Tree for containing your journey.
- Return to your sacred space – both of you! Spend a few moments there pondering your journey. Discuss it with your familiar – they will help you remember and know it *in your bones.*
- Find yourselves in Thisworld, lying together under your blanket again.
- Don't get up immediately. Turn on one side and curl up in the foetal position for a few minutes; your familiar will likely curl up with you, to help you. Gently recall, in your mind's eye, where you have been, who you have met, what gifts you have given and received. This is bringing home the goods, you need to tell over to yourself what you have done, seen, given and got so you remember it when you return to Thisworld.
- You are also reclaiming your body, getting to know and feel it again after you have been journeying out of it for half

an hour. You need to greet your body and thank it for still being there for you to come back to – don't take it for granted!

- When you are ready, gently sit up, then get up.
- Make any notes you want to, with your familiar.
- Close the Interface.
- Eat and drink to replace the physical energy you have used and to anchor yourself in your body again, and clear your space.

Do the follow-up ritual each morning and evening twilight for the three days *after* the journey.

Have something to drink and a snack to nibble, with your familiar.

Don't forget to clean up after yourself as usual!

This is a period of digestion, absorption and gestation so silence is the watch-word. Do *not* tell your experience abroad to all your friends but hold it sacred and secret within yourself or else you will abort it or give it premature birth.

12

Ancestors

What are the Ancestors?

Ancestors are those who've gone before us. They may be spirits, they may also have been incarnate as humans, but not always; they likely will have been incarnate as animals, plants, rocks, minerals and the bones of the Earth. Our Ancestors are everything that lives and moves and has its being not only on our Earth, but also throughout the cosmos.

People commonly think Ancestors are the physical bloodline of your current incarnation, but this isn't so. In order to learn and grow and help the Earth we've all been many things, many races, colours, creeds ... and many different species; and we will be again. We're not confined to only incarnating as humans, and certainly not to one particular family.

For the awenydd, their family is their spirit-group, the group with which they work across the worlds. This may – or may not – include members of their current blood-family.

As you know in archaeological terms human beings are the newest species on planet Earth, we're new boy on the block, so *everything* else in creation is our Ancestor, our Elder Brother.

Following the deer trods means learning this and learning all we can from our Ancestors.

Amergin/Taliesin tells us about being everything in his poem ...

The Song of Amergin
Translated by Robert Graves

I have been a stag of seven tines, running
I have been a flood across a wide plain, flowing

I have been a wind over a deep lake, whispering
I have been a tear from the brilliant sun, glistening
I have been a hawk in my nest above the cliff, watching
I have been a wonder among the lovliest flowers, blooming
I have been a god with smoke to fill the head, blazing
I have been a spear that roars for blood, flying
I have been a salmon in a clear pool, swimming
I have been a hill where poets walk, singing
I have been a boar upon the hills ruthless and red, roving
I have been a breaker from the winter sea, thundering
I have been a tide of the ocean, delivering to death and
returning...
Who, but I, knows the secrets of the unhewn dolmen?

I am the womb of every holt,
I am the blaze on every hill,
I am the queen of every hive,
I am the shield for every head,
I am the tomb of every hope...
Who, but I, gives birth to all that was, is and shall be?

All of the things that he has been enable him to *know* how their lives are, how they think, how they feel, how it is to be them. It's a form of shapeshifting and the ultimate way of learning for the awenydd. Shapeshifting is a dangerous and difficult art, which the awenydd learns after much previous study – we are not going into this in this book. If you want to go that far, to really learn, then you need a teacher in Thisworld who will help and mentor you through it.

This simple exercise will help bring you closer to the Ancestors.

Walks ...

Go for a walk and ask your familiar to be with you.

When you come to a place that pings in your spirit stop for a while; it may be a rock, tree, water, an animal den or tracks, or just a beautiful view.

Spend a moment to open the Interface.

When you are on the thread sit with whatever it is for a while.

Ask it to tell you about itself and about its Ancestors, and about those who were there before it too. You will be thrilled by the information you get.

You may be asked for help, or to do something. *Never* say yes straight away! Always ask for more information. If you feel you can be useful – and check with your familiar on this too – then talk with whoever it is about what needs to be done and what you are actually able to do. Keep you familiar well in the loop here!

If all is OK then agree. Otherwise say you are sorry, but you're really not up for this. You can add that you will remember what you've been told and if you find anyone else who may be able to help then you'll tell them about it.

Make notes of all that happens and spend time pondering – with your familiar – on the experience.

When you are done, close the Interface and either carry on your walk or go home.

13

Deer Folk

Who are the Deer Folk?

Deer Folk are the peoples of the Boreal Forest. The kinship of the Deer Folk is very wide and includes all the peoples who live in what was once the Boreal Forest. The Boreal Forest is the world of the reindeer, they thrive there. It is the land of Elen of the Ways for she is the goddess of the North Wind.

The Boreal Forest is the largest forest on Earth making up 29 percent of the world's forest. It extends all around the northern end of the world from the Tundra at latitude 70° to the southern tip of Cornwall at latitude 50°. Britain was part of the Boreal Forest, our old woods like the Caledonian forest, the moors and wild places in Wales and England, and the Highlands of Scotland, are all that's left. Its name comes from the ancient Greeks who called the North Wind Boreas. They called Britain *Hyperborea*, meaning *the land behind the North Wind* so we British were the *Hyperboreans*.

For us here in Britain the Deer Folk are our spirit-group, our clan, our spirit-home. This is a non-physical kinship connection that may also include members of your current bloodline. But physical blood is not the root, spirit is.

As you'll see in my book, *Elen of the Ways*, there are and have been Deer Folk throughout the Boreal Forest. Some still follow the reindeer in the old hunter-gatherer ways like the Caribou folk of the North-Western American continent, the Tsaatan reindeer herders of Northern Mongolia and the Sami people of Scandinavia.

Our own British traditions are only gradually coming to light here again. Archaeologists have found a few deer caves like those at Inchnadamph by the Meadows of the Stags in Scotland,

and some drawings like the one I described at the beginning that was found in South-West Wales. Mostly our ways have come down through word of mouth, families, songs, old mummers' plays and stories.

Unless you write or draw or carve on stone or bone most other things will rot away and decompose themselves back into their component atoms in a few years … let alone a few hundred thousand years. Add to that that much of our heritage was desecrated by Christians in the attempt to put us down and exterminate us and you can see why there is not much left. What is there has to be carefully picked out of ruins and brought to light by those of us whose families have held with the old ways over the centuries.

So we must go to tradition, story and song to find our way.

There are deer stories everywhere. Some of the best documented are those collected by JG McKay in his travels about the Highlands of Scotland that I talk about in *Elen of the Ways*. McKay believed there was a deer cult throughout Europe, it was wider than ever he thought as it ran and runs throughout the Boreal Forest.

We, too, had stories of deer-women and sometimes some of us could see them; they were the wise women of our village, working with our local spirit of place and with Elen of the Ways. I remember this from early childhood in the farm above Bittaford on the southern side of Dartmoor, later on the tors above Okehampton and later still on Exmoor. My family were part of it. I carry it all forward in the work now.

It's important to recognise that blood is not necessarily at all significant in the spirit-family ties we have with our relations. As I've said, blood relations may, or may not, be in the same spirit-clan(s) as you, and you may be in more than one clan yourself. When I was growing up, my favourite uncle was a woodsman and a *cunning man*; he taught me so much about the wild and the non-human world as well as the worlds of the Faer. I always called him uncle, still do, and felt incredibly close to him, closer even than to my father, but he was actually no blood-relation at all. He was brother of my father's first wife. He chose me out of the local children, above his own children and his sister's children, to take with him as apprentice. He was wonderful and amazing; I've never forgotten what he showed me. He was part of the same spirit group as me and of the same group as my dad although, again, there was no blood-tie between them.

Of course there was a blood-tie as well as a spirit tie between myself and my dad, who also taught me so much, and with my mother too; I only knew her in this world for the first three years of my life but I remember her well. She and my dad were of the same spirit-group, but of course there was no blood tie between them.

The animal group who led us into knowing the wisdom of the Earth, the solar system and the cosmos is what in other cultures is called the totem. This animal will be the Elder who has chosen to work with these peoples. They are part of our roots. All shamans from every tradition know they need to go back to their roots. The roots, in the tradition I follow, are the deer, Elen of the Ways, the antlered deer lady. She is our guardian-spirit.

She is very willing to impart her wisdom to us – thank the gods! We work through the spirits of the Deer Folk, our family, and so come to the wisdom … this is why we call it following the deer trods.

My family, spirit and physical, are all of the Deer Folk and have followed the deer trods for more generations than I can count without a lot of thinking. If you want to know more and deeper look on my website … www.elensentier.co.uk.

Moon Books invites you to begin or deepen your encounter with
Paganism, in all its rich, creative, flourishing forms.